(c) Copyright 2025, Freedom Philosophy

All rights reserved.
No part of this publication may be reproduced, distributed, or transmitted in any form, without the prior written permission of the publisher. Small parts of this work may be referenced and quoted under under fair use legislation, provided it is clearly attributed to the author.

Bulk orders may be placed by contacting the author:
Tel/SMS: +61 416243242
Online: www.freedomphilosophy.life

Printed in Australia

Publisher's Cataloging-in-Publication data
Visser-Marchant, Cornelis PJ
New Perspectives: a fresh look at common spiritual topics / Cor Visser-Marchant.
168p. 14 x 21cm.

Legal deposit with archives of National Library of Australia and State Library of Queensland. Free or discounted deposits with other libraries considered upon written request.

ISBN 978-0-6450743-4-5 (Paperback)
1. Spirituality and Faith - Philosophy - Spiritual Philosophy.
2. Religion - Christianity - Spiritual Christianity.

First Edition

Unless indicated otherwise, scripture references are from the New King James Version®. Copyright © 1982 by Thomas Nelson. Used by permission. All rights reserved.

New Perspectives

*A fresh look at
common spiritual topics*

Written by

Cor Visser-Marchant

My Gratitude and Dedication

I must offer my gratitude to my mother who is now passed away, my wife Sally and my three wonderful children Jeremy, Jasper and Holly, without whom I could not have grown into the person I am today. Despite the battles and hardship of life, I will be forever grateful for the love and support that I have received and continue to. It is this that has allowed me to dedicate my time and effort to this work. They are examples of living a true spiritual faith and in so doing support and inspire others.

I am dedicating this book to spiritual seekers: those who seek all that is good and true everywhere, those who walk the way of truth, those who acknowledge objective reality and all that entails, the ones who seek to understand the Infinite source of all that is and in whom, who is without time and space, we are all equal and united. Most of all, this work is dedicated to those who understand that changing the world is to change oneself from within and for whom freedom, integrity and peace are fundamental principles of life.

"seek first the kingdom of God and His righteousness, and all these things shall be added to you"

Matthew 6:33

Why this book?

*I*n this book, which I have called *New Perspectives*, I like to share with you new ways of looking at a range of spiritual concepts. Almost all of these perspectives deal with common philosophical or spiritual ideas. The approach to these, as you will discover, is somewhat different to common religious thought and many will actually defy popular beliefs.

Much of the philosophical basis of the ideas shared in this book are founded on, or grounded in, the spiritual philosophy revealed by Emanuel Swedenborg (1688-1772). His ideas have influenced many influential and well known people across the centuries, like Carl Jung, Helen Keller, Arthur Conan Doyle, James Tyler Kent, Norman Vincent Peale, Franklin Roosevelt and many others. (see https://freedomphilosophy.life/tributes-to-swedenborg/)

The important thing to note is that these ideas rise beyond our sense based thinking and lift our perspective up onto a higher level of spirituality and reason. I thank you for being open to take the time and find out differing ways to look at the world. I know you will find this book helpful for your own personal spiritual journey whatever your current beliefs may be.

> *"You shall know the truth, and the truth shall make you free."*
>
> *John 8:32*

Table of Content

Why this book?	... v
Building Resilience	... 9
Freedom from Religion	... 16
Creation	... 25
The Lord	... 29
The Word	... 35
Allegory and Symbolism	... 39
Faith	... 46
Truth	... 51
Wisdom	... 56
Good and Evil	... 59
Judgement	... 65
Forgiveness	... 68
Prayer	... 72
Love	... 75
Peace	... 78
Charity	... 81
The Neighbour	... 88
Humanity	... 91
Spirituality	... 96
Spiritual Growth	... 99
Christianity	... 103
Spiritual Christianity	... 107
The Church	... 110
Freedom	... 114
Male and Female	... 118
Marriage	... 122
Heaven and Hell	... 127
Innocence	... 134

New Perspectives

Happiness	... 139
The Golden Rule	... 144
Time	... 149
3 Keys to Spiritual Growth	... 152
How to read the Bible	... 159

Building Resilience

"To him who overcomes I will give some of the hidden manna to eat. And I will give him a white stone, and on the stone a new name"
Revelation 2:17

To start off, and before we discuss the various topics, I like to reflect a little on resilience and how to build it. The first thing to acknowledge is that life is hard, often seemingly unfair and many of us experience times of hardship and mental struggle. However relative the circumstances are, people's struggles are real and I hope this message may in some way help.

The reason why I want to start here, is because learning new truths, and so spiritual growth, is hard and difficult. The reason for this is that it separates us from who we were and it immediately separates us from what we thought we knew and were comfortable with. In other words, it takes us out of our comfort zone and forces us to become a different person! This is inevitable, because new knowledge cannot be unknown and so our reference point automatically shifts. This in turn shifts our relationship with the world and people around us, and more importantly shifts our relationship with our own view of self. In a sense, a little bit of us dies and something new replaces it and our character becomes fuller in the process.

Years ago, I suffered clinical depression and was medicated for it. This went on for a very long time and I can only say that it was terrible being that disconnected from my environment, family and friends. However, none of the medication, support and counselling actually cured or changed it. For me, I had to realise that I myself needed to change my thinking. I realised that, ultimately, I was responsible for my own mind and the only one that could actually make real changes to my thinking and thus the way I approached and experienced life. There was - and is - no magic pill.

I think that is such an important lesson to learn for all of us. That ultimately you are the only one in charge of your own mind and life. As parents we know that our children will go through hardship and come across experiences and opinions of others that are uncomfortable. We ourselves find out we are not so perfect and need to come to terms with the need to improve and shed some terrible and destructive habits. No person is exempt from that!

Therefore the best preparation is for individuals, while growing up, to be progressively exposed to the world and learn to stand up for themselves. Because sheltering our children from themselves and reality, will not allow them to learn the mental tools to become resilient, useful and dependable human beings capable of having their own rational will or purposeful intent. Exposure and practise is the only mechanism to build resilience and avoid a permanent state of victim-hood.

Let me also give you, from my perspective, and at risk of overly simplifying things somewhat, a great lesson I have learnt through my life experience. This is particularly aimed at those who are suffering states of anxiety or depression:

First is that you do have a choice even though it's really hard now or seems impossible or improbable to grasp and accept. As said before, only - and I mean only - you can determine what thoughts you accept and how you want to live your life. I understand the difficulties, but that is the harsh reality I found out for myself. We are not our thoughts and I will say a little more on that later.

The second is that dwelling on the past can really cause anger and depression through resentment, while fretting about what not yet is, is definitively unhelpful and often creates states of anxiety. More importantly, it takes us away from the ability to be present in the current moment - the only moment that is real and where joy can be experienced.

About the past

The immediate logical conclusion, of course, is to realise that there is no way you can change the past. No matter how much you wish it to have been different, you're going have to accept it!

That acceptance needs to come in two ways I believe:
1. There's no way you can hop into a time-machine and travel back in time - rescuing yourself from whatever it is that is keeping you trapped in your emotional or mental prison.
2. And if you're not happy where you are at, you can, and should, make choices to change that going forward. But, if your happy where you are now, then you also - in truth - really need to accept the past (not that that is a choice), because it has shaped the path to your current situation.

It will change the mental perception where you find yourself today.

Often this kind of thinking is tied with blaming, judging or criticising others. It is actually making you feel depressed, helpless and defeated. Ultimately it condemns us to defeat, because the past cannot be changed. And neither can you actually change another person.

So if you believe certain things about what other people think about you, or how their actions and intentions have affected you - whether true or not - you need to let it go.

About the future

If you look at the future - these things that haven't happened yet and may never ever actually happen either - you need to realise that nothing is ironclad and none of us control reality to make the future certain. The more you spent mental time there, the more you risk becoming really anxious, let alone reduce your ability to actually engage in the present and enjoy the moment.

You are setting yourself up for disappointment too, if things ultimately do not work out as you had planned. Again, this fretting is unhelpful and will always cause unnecessary angst. You shouldn't worry, feel threatened or be anxious about things you can't control, because that is seriously unhelpful. In fact, it is destructive and nothing good can ever come out of that sort of thinking. Only productive positive change can help.

You can't make any positive change or be useful in the past or future, you can only be useful now. Its only when you are present in the moment - right now - that you are able to be immersed in being, able to relax and be content. This, of course, is easier said than done, but recognising the truth of it is the first step.

Resilience comes only through practise

If you have a problem with your emotions and your thoughts you need to learn how to deal with them. You must cast off the unwanted thoughts, such as depression, self-aggrandisement, egotism, et cetera, in order to have control over your mind. The only way healing from mental anguish comes about, is by taking responsibility and exerting control over your mind. Nobody else is able to do it for you.

When you have control, you have a choice of practically engaging with the emotions and thoughts you take on, accept and dwell on, in that sense then you do have the actual power to choose. This leads to one very helpful realisation and truth that I can offer to you: YOU ARE NOT YOUR THOUGHTS.

However hard that may seem, thoughts aren't physical and they aren't part of you unless you make them so. The same goes with feelings. Thoughts and feelings come and go, which make it obvious that they are not you, so allow me to offer you the following propositions:

- We are not our thoughts and feelings, but these flow into us. We don't have conscious control of these coming in - they are not part of us. Emanuel Swedenborg - a 17th century philosopher - calls this *influx*.
- We can, and must, however, reflect on these thoughts and feelings and decide which thoughts and affections to hold on to and own and which to reject, because the thoughts and affections underpin our behaviour, our deeds and words and so shape our character.

So many people seem to identify with their feelings and emotions as if these make them who they are. Well, doing so puts you immediately into a perpetual state of victimhood - being at the mercy of the thoughts and feelings flowing in, without the ability to control them. How can you have any freedom and peace of mind, when you are held ransom to your thoughts and feelings - being unable to determine your own course of action? I want to urge you against such thinking, because that is where we end up either depressed or anxious or both.

Those who choose not to own or reject their feelings and emotional responses - or are never forced to - develop within themselves a lack of resilience and an inability to control themselves. This then leads to them expecting that everybody else must be controlled. The weird thing is, there are people who actually believe this. They cannot see that not everyone can work around and accommodate to everyone else unless we become homogenous automatons.

We cannot expect the world to acknowledge and accept our way of life and behaviour without compromise, question or criticism. This position is especially hypocritical when we ourselves are out of control and behave without compromise or consideration of the needs of others. I have noticed that those who believe such, also see a rejection of their feelings and attitudes as a rejection of them as a person - their personhood itself. Which is a very unhealthy way to think indeed.

Another way to express it is to say that if you're not in control of your thoughts (and so too your feelings) you immediately become a kind of victim. A victim (or perhaps better: slave) of your thoughts, which immediately flows to not having any control over any impulses of your actions, because your emotions and your feelings, the ones you choose to accept, engage with, are the ones that drive the value behind your action and its physical response.

That's a really dangerous place to be in, and in terms of rationality, turns you into some kind of animalistic or inhuman state. You are removing the sapient element from the homo sapiens. Just acting on our impulse, removes our rationality and that is ultimately dehumanising. We can't blame anybody else but ourselves, because that is where we find the control centre of our mental state.

I may also, just make a brief side note here that perfectionism and being too demanding of yourself is equally unhealthy and unrealistic. Such idealistic thinking sets your mind up to fail also, because such approach is ever incremental and places us into thinking nothing is never good enough. I can attest to this too from personal experience.

> *"Whoever comes to Me, and hears My sayings and does them ... is like a man building a house, who dug deep and laid the foundation on the rock. And when the flood*

arose, the stream beat vehemently against that house, and could not shake it, for it was founded on the rock. But he who heard and did nothing is like a man who built a house on the earth without a foundation, against which the stream beat vehemently; and immediately it fell."

Luke 6:46-49

Freedom from Religion

"Take heed and beware of the leaven of the Pharisees and the Sadducees."

Matthew 16:6

I like to assert to you, that the reason religion is in the 'cool-room' and its overall perception in the decline, is that most of the time, perhaps almost all of the time, religious ideas, rules or principles are 'man-made' and they restrict or inhibit actual spiritual growth in a person. That is a big statement, but bear with me to explain.

Let me begin by saying that I am not advocating that there are no rules to abide by or that all rules are evil, nor that those imposing the rules have bad intent. In fact, having firm rules in place, like the Ten Commandments, is useful and good, especially for those who are young and immature or still learning and trying to understand. They are there, like a safety net, to minimise harm and in place to protect and guide, rather than to dominate and control, and as one of those imposing such rules - I like to believe - most come from a place of caring usefulness and love to the neighbour. In the same way most parents care for their children.

Rules are in place to protect, but once their reasoning and the potential consequences of not following these same rules are understood, then it's no longer appropriate or right to enforce that behaviour and to dominate and control that person, because then they can, and must, own that for themselves and therefore the consequences as well.

See, spiritual growth, or affecting positive change in ones inner character and life, - the purpose of religion -

cannot happen by osmosis. Therefore the blind following of rules doesn't help unless it is the first step of understanding their reasoning and purpose.

I think this is a crucial point to understand, but also self-evident, as highlighted in this quote from Emanuel Swedenborg (1688-1772).

> *"Everyone recognises that none of us can be compelled to think what we do not want to think, or to intend what we do not want to intend. So we cannot be compelled to believe what we do not believe, and certainly not anything that we do not want to believe, or to love what we do not love, and certainly not anything that we do not want to love."*
>
> Divine Providence 129

And it goes on to say:

> *"Our spirit or mind has complete freedom to think, intend, believe, and love. This freedom comes to us by an inflow from the spiritual world, which does not compel us. Our spirit or mind is actually in that world.*
> *We can be compelled to say that we think and intend something, or that we believe and love something, but unless this is or becomes a matter of our own desire and consequent reasoning, it is not something that we really think, intend, believe, and love."*
>
> Ibid.

For example...

> *"We can also be compelled to speak in favour of religion, and to act according to a religion, but we cannot be compelled to think in its favour as a matter of our own faith and to intend it as a matter of our own love."*
>
> Ibid.

I believe there is a warning in there for us and I like to unpack a few elements from it.

The first is that inner (character) transformation comes from the inside out. Everything comes from the inside out. The spiritual world is first, while the natural is the world of consequences. However, we constantly tend to act as if this world is going to change our mind or spirit. "If only a person behaves like this on Sunday...", we say; "If we only have the worship service in this format...", "If we only teach this...", "If they only believe this...", "Then", we think; "they will be perfect", "they'll be spiritual", "they'll be saved", "they will go to heaven".

While we must interact in this world, I think such focus on the external aspects is dangerous and potentially counter-productive. I think it is indisputable that a person has to change their own thinking, their own affection, about what they can accept and receive within their own mind. That is what ultimately changes them externally. The internal changes and external will fall into line with our internal, not the other way around. That is the lesson!

Merely having compliance with behavioural rules simply produces external compliance, but unless it is done so voluntarily - fully - it can simply produce resentment and cause the opposite effect.

Part of our humanity is that we can behave differently on the outside than we feel or think on the inside. For example, we can go to church, while disliking it. I grew up in a mostly Protestant country, and I think, like most Protestant countries, with prior generations everybody went to church on Sundays, even more so in smaller communities. I don't believe there were many that dared not to go to church on a Sunday. You know, everybody filed in, in their best dress, on Sunday.

Life was a little different. The church was in the middle of the village. The church had power, it had control: it was the central hub of life for most. And of course, that represents a good thing. That is, in essence, a good thing, but the peer pressure, that kind of external control....is something else!

People had to go to church: there was no freedom not to go. To force them to go to church is not a good thing. When you're forced to do something - ask any teenager - you tend to rile up against it, and you start rejecting it.

Well, the lesson there is, is that while you're in that space of mind to reject that compulsion you are not in a position to accept the rule freely. That is the danger of compulsion! Swedenborg gives us another lovely passage expressing it:

> *"the seed that is sown in freedom lasts, but what is sown under compulsion does not, because compulsion is not in accordance with the person's will, but with the will of the one who compels."*
>
> New Jerusalem and Its Heavenly Doctrine 143

If you're forced to study or read the Bible, you're going to be in a state of apprehension and rejection, are you not? Again, for a child there are benefits in memorising some of those stories, because there's so much power in them, but once you're an adult you have to just learn and think about it for yourself. If you're going to have to read it - if you're forced to read it every single day - it lacks the benefit, because that isn't transformative. In fact, it likely does the opposite.

So while religion enforces specific rules, spiritual growth actually requires freedom, because inner transformation requires our own affection and personal choice. We can only learn and be receptive when we actually choose so, voluntarily. We must apply our heart and mind fully if we are to effect character change.

> *"Everyone who knows and lives according to them [the Ten Commandments], not merely from the civil and moral*

> *law, but also from the Divine law, will be saved; thus everyone in his own religion, whether Christian, or Mohammedan, or Gentile."*
>
> *Apocalypse Explained 1179*

Here, Swedenborg is unequivocally clear that, regardless of a person's belief system (ie religion), provided that they accept that there is a Divine and the humility to accept an objective reality - whatever that may be - that they can be instructed and can become wise.

There are some inherent moral rules that come out of that, which I have to abide by. The Ten Commandments basically encapsulate those fundamentals: that life is fundamental, you don't kill a person, you don't lie, and don't steal, and the like. It doesn't have to be the exact same rules: just having a code of conduct that comes out of a belief system that is applied with integrity to their lives.

That's all it requires, to live with integrity, because people that do that have the humility to accept truth as it really is. They'll have the humility to accept objective reality when it is presented to them in a way that they can accept it. ... And maybe we're not in any position to give it to them.

At the very least, we ought to really understand why we believe what we believe. If you don't understand why you believe what you believe, than why are you doing it? Clearly, you have to test yourself, and to live what you believe, and understand that from practice, so you can share it with others. We should be able to explain why we believe what we believe, because we've tested the fundamental basis for it and say:"I know why I believe it, and I live what I believe and I understand what I believe, and so I can explain it to you." This is incumbent upon all of us to be able to do, but you cannot put yourself in a position that says; "I will teach you what you should believe."

"But you, do not be called Rabbi, for one is your teacher, the Christ, and you're all brethren."
Matthew 23:8

Basically, Christ is very clearly saying I am the only one that teaches. I am the Word. I am reality and truth. I am the door. I'm the shepherd. I'm the vine. Over and over, and over, and over, and over ... The way. So the only way a person, us, any and all of us, can learn, according to scripture is God in them opening up their understanding ever progressively.

It's not us, even though we try and offer help, and, that's because we have that apparent autonomy in life. Through sharing what we know, we learn as well. But there's a big difference with us wanting to share what we have from a good place - it's a whole other thing altogether to share from a place of judgement and thinking, I'm in an elevated spiritual state because I know more.

You see the difference? You have to be so very careful.

Compulsion is evil and dangerous

Now over a hundred years ago they were already wanting to do compulsory vaccinations and there was an uproar, uproar; "Down with compulsion!", and rightfully so. Not that I wish to focus on the health industry, but what I want to try to get to here is that if God can come to us, where we are at - and He calls us by our name - then why can we be so definitive about what one must believe, what religious dogma and vocabulary one must use and comply with?

I wholeheartedly believe that every single person ever in history, and everywhere in the world now, has an equal opportunity to fulfil their spiritual potential. We're all unique, you know? We're not all the same. And all the externals, the appearances of knowledge, and the appearances of skills, and IQ, and all of that-- that's just that - appearance. We don't really need that. It's all people equally, everywhere, have that potential, because God is equally with all of them.

Now, that brings us, too, to the Word, and what the Word is, when we talk about a select number of books in the Word. Well, in my opinion that is wrong, but more on that later.

The Word is creation. It is where good and truth come into effect. That's what the Word is, because it's from God and is God. And so, teaching that you find elsewhere, if we compare teaching to teaching, then you will find sections in the Q'uran, sections in the Bhagavad Ghita, sections in other ancient teachings, that are all the Word, because it all leads back and points back to God, and is from God.

So if you go to the Middle East, or if you go to Nepal, the Bible may mean little or nothing to them. You can't expect them to accept it on face value, because there is no match in the thinking, in the understanding, in the way of life. It's so different, so foreign to them that you are not going to break that barrier down.

I think the fundamental equaliser is living the precepts of one's own religion, by having the humility to accept objective reality as it really is.

What I'm trying to say, is that when we get onto our high horse and say, hey, you know, our religion is the best and therefore we'll be saved. We immediately fail. You understand what I mean?

There's a difference between having a higher level of knowledge or wisdom perhaps. But that doesn't mean you're better in a spiritual place, right? If you have a different vocabulary, a different range of words to describe reality, and you have a different way of understanding it. So I think in that sense, when you try and when we deal with others, we should always got to try and deal with what is of God in them.

What about atheists?

Believe it or not, atheists have their beliefs. Atheism is a religion in itself, too. You have preset rules that you have to follow, or ideas you have to accept, which is what religion is, then you get into trouble, right? So it is no different for them and this applies to all of us.

Some will be very forthcoming and say, hey; "I'm actually an anti-theist - I'm against God", and obviously they mean their idea of God. The underlying fundamental principle that distinguishes those that believe from those that don't believe in a deity is the placing of self in a position of God and autonomy, or not.

That is, basically, the distinguishing factor between being able to accept God, and not. Because at the heart of it is that you put yourself in place of ultimate power and you think yourself better because you're smart and clever, and you understand much, and if you've got that arrogance: what then is the inspiration for you to do that inner reflection, the introspection and to motivation to change yourself?

And where does that guiding principle come from, that morality. So some are agnostic. But they're still focusing on self.

Some people can't accept Jesus Christ because they think He was just a man, and there's a lot of doubt. But rejecting a creator, an intelligent creator—that's a whole different thing. That is the ultimate source of self-aggrandisement and spiritual doom.

Well, it's the inner principle, within you, that's where

it comes from, - your love - and you either have a love for what is good and true or you have a love for self. Those are the absolute ultimate extremes that you operate from. If you come from a love of self, everything you do, think and believe operates and rests on that love of self and seeks to serve it. That is rejecting objective reality as we understand it. Now, when you're going through all sorts of contortions and idea twisting of reality to make it fit this love of self and rejection of God, to me, is crazy.

These are the babblers, they use big words and complicated ideas, and people get bamboozled by it, because all of a sudden nothing is not quite nothing, or alternate realities, alien crystals, or time as an actor. Redefining something to suit a different purpose.

Swedenborg says that you can't actually recognise see what is non-sensical unless you have an elevated understanding. And you can't get the enlightenment unless you're willing to learn and accept what reality is.

If you put God first, the use first, objective reality, what is good and what is true first and foremost, loving your neighbour and you put that as a first principle that underpins and supports everything else, then you can see your place in that, your function and what you can do. This too is a love of self in a proper sense.

Now let us proceed...

Creation

"I am the Lord, who makes all things."

Isaiah 44:24

Many people see creation as a coincidental by product of an explosion from nothing with a magical process of natural evolution possibly triggered by alien crystal based lifeforms

OR

they think of a sky based Divine being as having started the process and continuing to observe it from a distance to keep a watchful eye.

I put it to you that both these ideas disregard basic scientific logic and are fundamentally flawed.

Today the scientific hypothesis of Darwinian single-cell origin evolution and a momentary Big Bang still prevails. Some people like Richard Dawkins even suggest that the first life-form could have arrived on this planet on the back of an alien crystal to kick start the entire process. Of course this position is absurd and does not answer the primal question of ultimate cause.

Some rather prefer a fantasy of billions of alternate universes that coexist and undetectable parallel dimensions over the idea of a single ultimate and intelligent source. This of course then turns science into its own weird religion in the process and moving away from fundamental principles of logic, measurement and observation.

Many faith-based traditions such as Christianity approach believe in an intelligent origin of *Creation*. You can even see it in indigenous spirituality, like Aboriginal Dreamtime. However most believe that there is some form of natural evolution process that occurs after the Divine has instigated or initiated a process, while there is no continual engagement by this Divine Creator in this evolutionary process and that we're fully guided by natural laws.

Now let me ask you a few basic questions:
- is inert matter - dead matter - capable of organising itself into a complex living structure?
- can something cause itself to come into existence? and
- can intelligent live spring from nothing?

In my opinion logic dictates that the answer to all three of these questions must must ultimately be no. One way or another we must accept some unseen prior cause for the existence of our universe and take it on faith, whether we are religious or not.

What is dead and without live cannot become alive by itself. What is inert and without any external force cannot gain momentum by itself. This is simply illogical. Any change requires an external force - an external influence - whether their conscious or not.

I often hear it said that probability increases over time, so that justifies the idea of increased likelihood. However, time is of course not a force and therefore cannot affect or effect anything. We will touch more on this topic later also.

Something cannot cause itself to come into existence from nothing. An effect can not at the same time be its own cause. Therefore something must have a prior cause.

> *People do say that the whole world was created out of nothing, and they like to think of "nothing" as absolutely nothing. However, nothing comes from "absolutely nothing" and nothing can. This is an abiding truth.*
> *Divine Love and Wisdom 55*

Now only intelligence is capable of order, which is

purposeful structure. Intelligence cannot come from nothing. Intelligence has to be acquired - this can only be acquired from a prior source of intelligence.

I want you, the reader, to just ignore for the moment the term "God". Park it aside for for now and focus instead on an ultimate reality, an ultimate source or prior cause from which we all have our being. In Latin it is called *a Priori*, which means without a prior cause, or "not caused" and effectively means the ultimate cause.

If you accept the logical conclusion of something requiring a prior effect, then you can only conclude that there must be an infinite source from which we all have our cause, and which in itself does not have a prior cause. This permanent causality, which maintains all its effects and intermediary causes constantly - including you as you are processing this information. If it were not so then there would be no Primum or cause *a priori*. There would not be a root cause and therefore no subsequent effects and therefore nothing at all.

Compare the life energy of our universe with electricity. If we stop producing electricity the energy stops and nothing works. Now not only must there be a constant source or energy that maintains our existence, but this power must also have intelligence. Given the order and structure of our reality, not to mention the intelligence that is obvious in us.

We will touch on it a bit more later, but Swedenborg provides an important insight:

> *"Nothing can exist anywhere in the material world that does not have a correspondence with the spiritual world —because if it did, it would have no cause that would make it come into being and then allow it to continue in existence. Everything in the material world is an effect. The causes of all effects lie in the spiritual world..."*
>
> Arcana Coelestia 5711

This provides us with a clear order in creation. Randomness and chaos are ultimately destructive and not constructive, so only purposeful order can be sustained indefinitely. If you think logically, you will see that chaos cannot produce permanent order.

Here is what Swedenborg says:

> *"People who think rationally and clearly see that the universe was not created from nothing because we see that nothing can arise from nothing. Nothing simply is nothing and to make something out of nothing is also self contradictory."*
>
> Divine Love and Wisdom 283.

Something cannot come from nothing, I hope you can see that.

Something cannot cause itself to come into existence, let alone from nothing, I hope you can see that too. And what is inert or dead - that what does not have life - cannot cause life or intelligence to come into existence.

Therefore the only conclusion that you can logically reach is that there must be an ultimate primal cause and that this primal cause must be without cause itself. Here is a nice quote to round this topic off with. It might be helpful to prelude it by explaining that the name Jehovah means: "is, was, (coming into) being".

> *"Jehovah God is Being in itself, because He is I am, the very, sole and prime source, from eternity to eternity, of everything in existence, which allows it to exist. In this and no other sense He is the Beginning and the End, the First and the Last, Alpha and Omega."*
>
> True Christian Religion 21

The Lord

"And the Word became flesh and dwelt among us, and we beheld His glory, the glory as of the only begotten of the Father, full of grace and truth."

John 1:14

When they hear the term "Lord" many people think of a person: a man in a robe, sandals on dusty feet, walking the hills of Galilee and eventually hanging on a cross. And while this may indeed reflect the natural manifestation of Jesus of Nazareth, I put it to you that the Lord is not a separate (read 'finite') person (or 'form') at all.

Instead, the Lord is the infinite Divine itself — ALL that which *is* Good and *is* True. That which made all things, sustains all things, and is present within all things. He is not just a man who once lived amongst men in time and space, but the eternal cause and force of Love and Wisdom, the very essence of Life itself. The Lord tells us Himself:

"Most assuredly, I say to you, before Abraham was, I AM."

John 8:58

And most clearly:

"I am the resurrection and the life."

John 11:25

If the Lord is Divine Wisdom, and if Divine Wisdom is what shapes, sustains and orders the universe — then the Lord is not simply a person in history. He is the source of all order, the harmony behind the cosmos, the intelligence within creation.

This Divine Wisdom is always united with Divine Love — for the two are inseparable. And together they form the very *life* of all that is:

> *"In Him was life, and the life was the light of men."*
>
> John 1:4

And:
> *"I and My Father are one."*
>
> John 10:30

Swedenborg explains that everything ...

> *"is arranged into its form and preserved in it by the Divine Love acting by means of the Divine Wisdom."*
>
> True Christian Religion 37

In the same chapter and throughout his writings, he explains that Life is Divine Love; and Light is Divine Wisdom. So then, the Lord is Life and Light — not in metaphor, but in literal spiritual truth.

He is not someone to believe in merely as a figure from the past. The Lord is the Love and Wisdom and purpose flowing into every person, every tree, every breath, every truth, every act of goodness.

Loving the Lord

We are told:

> *"You shall love the Lord your God with all your heart, all your soul, and all your mind"*
>
> Matthew 22:37

But how is this done?

The answer lies in understanding *what* the Lord actually is. He is not merely Jesus the man, but the Divine made flesh — the *Word*, the *Life*, the *Light* — the infinite *Good* and *Truth* made present in the world. To love the Lord, then, is to love goodness itself. To cherish truth. To honour love in action.

Swedenborg writes:

> *"In heaven, 'loving the Lord' does not mean loving him for the image he projects, but loving the good that comes from him."*
>
> Heaven and Hell 15

To love good, as we will touch on later in more detail, is to will and do good. This aligns beautifully with what we explore in the other chapters. To love the Lord is to align ourselves with the reason behind creation — which is Love itself.

In this sense, the Lord is not something *out there*, but the internal aim and purpose of life itself. He is the good you try to live out. He is the truth you seek to understand. He is the love you feel when you forget yourself and give without condition.

> *"God is Love, and he who abides in love abides in God, and God in him."*
>
> 1 John 4:16

As we explored in the chapter on *Creation*, nothing can come from nothing. There must be a primal cause — not just a cause that once acted in the distant past, but one that is ever present, sustaining all things indefinitely. That Cause is the Lord. Not only because He is the First, but because He is the *only* — the very Being and Life behind all other beings and life.

And this Being, the Divine, took on human form to make itself known to us — to become accessible, relatable, even personal. This is what is meant by the Word becoming flesh. It is not that God changed into a man, but rather that the infinite entered the finite minds, so that we could see with our eyes, hear with our ears, and understand with our hearts what Love and Wisdom look like in real life.

> *"He who has seen Me has seen the Father."*
>
> *John 14:9*

What, then, does it mean to truly love the Lord?
- It is not to love a picture in a church.
- It is not to worship a name.
- It is not to believe in a doctrine.
- It is not even to accept a story as historical fact.

To love the Lord is to love the eternal — to love what is good because it is Good, to love what is true because it is True, and to allow these to shape who we are and what we do.

> *"The Lord is near to all who call on Him, to all who call on Him in truth."*
>
> *Psalm 145:18*

Thus, to love the Lord is to will what is good, to understand what is true, and to act from that union. It will become clear as you explore the other chapters, that this is the very definition of heaven in us: it is a love that transcends personality and reaches into eternity.

And when we live from that centre — when we love the neighbour, act justly, and seek wisdom with a sincere and humble heart — we are loving the Lord, whether we know it or not.

The one who does not change!

Before we move on, though, I like you to ponder on the following important verses:

> *"For I am the Lord, I do not change."*
>
> *Malachi 3:6*

> *Jesus Christ is the same yesterday, today, and forever.*
>
> *Hebrews 13:8*

> *"I am the Alpha and the Omega, the Beginning and the End," says the Lord, "who is and who was and who is to come, the Almighty."*
>
> *Revelation 1:8*

Now take your understanding that the infinite is eternally the same and must be without the same character flaws as us. This must be so, because infinite means without end and so without boundary and without form. Add to this the knowledge that life, and so reality, is *Spirit* not - "here" or "there" - physical.

How then do we marry the spiritual with the physical experience? How then do we 'see' the infinite?

Consider it is only we that are capable of change and progress: in fact we must change, and do so, as a result of growing in understanding. We shape ourselves through the choices we make - something the Divine cannot do or force! Everything that is is already in the Source - all potentiality - is for our benefit.

What changes is how it is received, perceived and acted on (responded to) and therefore how our filtering shapes our reality and experience. Ponder on this and then perceive our role in projecting our experiential reality.

> *"Assuredly, I say to you, inasmuch as you did it to one of the least of these My brethren, you did it to Me."*
> *Matthew 25:40*

The Word

> *"In the beginning was the Word, and the Word was with God, and the Word was God. He was in the beginning with God. All things were made through Him, and without Him nothing was made that was made."*
>
> John 1:1–3

When people hear the phrase *The Word*, most instinctively think of the Bible. Some even consider the printed book itself to be sacred in and of its pages, as if the physical ink on its physical paper held some kind of supernatural essence.

But I suggest it to you that The Word is not the Bible - and the Bible is not The Word.

Certainly, the Bible is a vessel — a finite container, if you will — that holds a representation of the Word, and to certain extent even corresponds with it, in time and space. But The Word, in its truest and most complete sense, is far more expansive. It is nothing less than what is of the Divine itself.

> *"In the beginning was the Word, and the Word was with God, and the Word was God."*
>
> John 1:1

> *"God is reality itself, and everything that exists must come from that reality."*
>
> Divine Love and Wisdom 55

Swedenborg tells us that "the Word" signifies Divine Truth — not just truth as a concept, but Truth as the very structure of all being. He writes:

> *"The Word is Divine truth itself, thus the Lord Himself. For the Lord is the Word because He is the Divine truth, and the Word is the Divine truth because it is from the Lord and concerning the Lord."*
>
> *Doctrine of the Sacred Scripture 1*

This means that everything which is in harmony with what is good and true - everything that arises from Divine Love and expresses Divine Wisdom — is the Word. The Word is the form, or structure, which Love takes when it manifests as thought, reason, creation, and purposeful order. It is the Divine intelligibility behind all things.

To say it plainly: The Word is reality itself — the Divine order, purpose, and wisdom from which, and by which, all things exist and continue to be.

To be clear, the Bible, at least those parts untainted by the author's own natural influence, is indeed sacred. It contains within it the living correspondence of the Divine — layers of meaning, historical narrative, spiritual allegory, and heavenly symbolism.

> *"And beginning at Moses and all the Prophets, He expounded to them in all the Scriptures the things concerning Himself.... And they said to one another, 'Did not our heart burn within us while He talked with us on the road, and while he opened the Scriptures to us?'"*
>
> *Luke 24:27,32*

Swedenborg calls this the internal sense of scripture, but these stories and verses only contain power to the extent they mirror what is real: to the extent they reflect the Divine pattern.

The book itself is not *The Word*. It bears witness to the Word. Just as the body is not the soul, the Bible is not God

— but it is the form in those parts of it in which Divine Wisdom can dwell when we read it with a loving and discerning heart.

> *"..although the style of the Word seems simple in the sense of the letter, it is such that nothing can ever be compared to it in excellence, since Divine wisdom lies concealed not only in the meaning as a whole but also in each word; and that in heaven this wisdom shines forth."*
>
> Heaven and Hell 310

Thus, when we treat the Bible as holy, it is not because of its external form but because of the Divine it points toward and contains within. Like a map to a hidden treasure, the value is not the paper and ink — it is what the map leads us to: a deeper knowledge of the Lord, and of the reality that flows from Him, allowing conjunction in us.

Let me offer you a fresh way to think of this:

The Word is not merely spoken or written. It is the order of life itself. It is the wisdom embedded in nature, the harmony found in conscience, the intelligence of usefulness, the inner voice that urges us toward love, truth, and selflessness. It is the tangible or visible form of Divine Love.

The Bhagavad Gita too speaks of this when Krishna says:

> *"I am the source of all spiritual and material worlds. Everything emanates from Me."*
>
> Bhagavad Gita 10:8

The Word, then, is the declaration of being — the utterance not of sound, but of Divine intention manifesting as *reality*.

To read the Word, then, is not limited to opening a book. It is also to observe reality rightly — to perceive what is good and true around us, to understand cause and effect, to see the image of the Divine in our neighbour, to recognise the laws of love and wisdom that hold the universe in place.

This also means that The Word is not a thing of the past. It is not a dead document. It is alive. It is happening *now*. You are living in it and surrounded by it.

> *"For the Word of God is living and powerful, and sharper than any two-edged sword..."*
>
> Hebrews 4:12

This is why the scriptures also say:

> *"Heaven and earth will pass away, but My words will by no means pass away."*
>
> Matthew 24:35

Because those words are not only on paper — they are the laws of spiritual life, the truths of Divine order, the principles of *Love* and *Wisdom* upon which the entire universe depends.

To live the Word is to live in accordance with reality. It is to speak truth and act from love. It is to seek what is useful, to harmonise with what is eternal, to follow the way of Good — regardless of personal gain. It is to live in such a way that our thoughts, intentions, and actions become a living scripture.

> *"to love truth is to will and do it."*
>
> Heaven and Hell 15

In other words: the Word becomes flesh not once, but every time you embody love and truth. Every time you speak or act from what is good and wise, *you* become a vessel of the Word, and this is how heaven is made — within us - and this is how we get our own Book of Life to reflect the Word.

Allegory and Symbolism

"And He opened their understanding, that they might comprehend the Scriptures."

Luke 24:45

Here I want to take a brief moment to reflect on the Ancient Symbolism and Allegory that can be found in the Sacred Scriptures. Without discarding the significance of congruent literal text, my focus is the Divine teachings within sacred scriptures, since these apply primarily and directly to the realm of our mind, individually and personally.

Let us have a look at what the Bible itself tells us:

"Open my eyes, that I may see wondrous things from Your law. I am a stranger in the earth, do not hide Your commandments from me."

Psalm 119:18,19

"..the words are closed up and sealed till the time of the end. ...none of the wicked shall understand, but the wise shall understand."

Daniel 12:9,10

"They shall run to and fro, seeking the word of the Lord, but shall not find it."

Amos 8:12

"He who has ears, let him hear! ....it has been given to you to know the mysteries of the kingdom of heaven, but to them is has not been given... Therefore I speak to

them in parables, because seeing they do not see, and hearing they do not hear, nor do they understand."

Matthew 13:9,11,13

"And beginning at Moses and all the Prophets, He expounded to them in all the Scriptures the things concerning Himself. .. And they said to one another, 'Did not our heart burn within us while He talked with us on the road, and while He opened the Scriptures to us?'"

Luke 24:27,32

"I still have many things to say to you, but you cannot bear them now. However, when He, the Spirit of truth, has come, He will guide you into all truth."

John 16:12-13

"These things I have spoken to you in figurative language.."

John 16:25

"..the letter kills, but the Spirit gives life."

2 Corinthians 3:6

"Tell me, you who desire to be under the law, do you not hear the law? ..which things are symbolic.."

Galatians 4:21,24

"..praying also for us, that God would open to us a door for the word, to speak the mystery of Christ.."

Colossians 4:3

"..the way into the Holiest of All was not yet made manifest while the first tabernacle was still standing. It was symbolic.."

Hebrews 9:8

> "Give ear, O my people, to my law; Incline your ears to the words of my mouth. I will open my mouth in a parable; I will utter dark sayings of old."
>
> Psalm 78:1,2

> "But even to this day, when Moses is read, a veil lies on their heart. Nevertheless when one turns to the Lord, the veil is taken away. Now the Lord is the Spirit; and where the Spirit of the Lord is, there is liberty."
>
> 2 Corinthians 3:15-17

This hidden treasure map to personal spiritual application can be found through the understanding of ancient symbolism if coupled with a sincere willingness to be led by truth from the Word on a quest to develop our true inner character.

Swedenborg tells us:

> "Read the Word, and believe in the Lord, and you will see the truths which should constitute your faith and life; for all in the Christian world draw their doctrine from the Word as from the only fountain. ... every man whose soul desires it is capable of seeing the truths of the Word in the light..., provided indeed he hungers after it, and seeks it from the Lord"
>
> Apocalypse Revealed 224

There are three fundamental assumptions to be understood which underpin Freedom Philosophy's approach to any scripture study and which should be understood clearly.

They are:

The Divine is the Source

The Divine is the *Source* of all wisdom, all love and therefore all truth and life! This is not limited to the physical and literal text of the books in the Bible. We can access and connect with the great **I AM** through opening our inner self, yearning to learn the truth and by seeking to serve others meaningfully. There are even many other great sacred texts that channel The Word and through which the Divine, Jehovah God, can teach and transform us.

> *"Religion has spread into the whole world from the ancient Word."*
>
> Divine Providence 254

Also from Emanuel Swedenborg:

> *"From His omnipotence God created the universe, and introduced order into each thing and all things in it ... God also preserves the universe, and unceasingly watches over the order of it with its laws; and when anything falls from order He brings it back and makes it whole again."*
>
> True Christian Religion 74

Our mind is not physical

We already operate with our mind in the spiritual realm. Some call it dream world, world of spirits or the metaphysical realm. It doesn't matter what you call it, the truth is that our thoughts and feelings originate from it and remain non-physical. We already connect with heaven right now, by developing a heavenly state of being within ourselves. Our ability to be transformed comes courtesy of the all-knowing source of all, through divine principles operating since the beginning of time.

> "Everything that is done according to Divine order is inwardly open to the Lord, and thus has heaven in it. Divine order is for the Lord to flow in through the interiors of man into his exteriors, thus through the will of man into his action. .. How a man must live for it to be according to order, the Word teaches..."
>
> Arcana Coelestia 8513

The external experience reflects our mind

The natural world and our experience within it, does not operate independently from our mind and the Divine, but in essence reflects the Divine through us. Because of this, our outer experience depends on our connection with God and can be traced back to those divine principles operative within the human mind.

> "Whatever in universal nature does not have correspondence with the spiritual world cannot exist, having no cause from which to exist, consequently from which to subsist. The things that are in nature are nothing but effects; their causes are in the spiritual world... Nor can the effect subsist unless the cause is constantly in it, because the effect ceases when the cause ceases. Regarded in itself the effect is nothing else than the cause, but so clothed outwardly as to enable the cause to act as a cause in a lower sphere. ... Hence it is also plain that as each and all things in the world have come forth from the Divine, they continue to come forth from the Divine."
>
> Arcana Coelestia 5711

The closer you look, the more everything is in harmony and a perfect representation of us. The symbolism within the Bible (and other sacred texts), ties perfectly back to the operation of the human mind and its associated states and qualities. This is where we find the understanding of the symbolism.

> "All things in The Word both in general and in particular, ... down to the most minute iota, signify and enfold within them spiritual and heavenly things.. that the Word is really of this character might be known from the single consideration that being the Lord's and from the Lord it must of necessity contain within it such things as belong to heaven ... and that unless it did so it could not be called the Lord's Word, nor could it be said to have any life in it. .....the Lord, who is the very Life itself."
>
> *Arcana Coelestia 2*

I believe the symbolism that is being discussed here was well understood in ancient times, but has since long been forgotten. We can trace remnants of it back within the oldest known languages, within myths, stories and even those sayings that have survived in the modern world. You only need to bring a humble state of mind: a willingness to be led by the Lord.

> "Speak what is high! high! Let what is ancient come out of your mouth"
>
> *1 Samuel 2:3*

> "I will utter dark sayings of old"
>
> *Psalms 78:2*

I promise, that once you start reading the Sacred Scriptures with these ancient keys revealed through allegory and symbolism, your understanding will open your inner world and your spiritual life will be transformed and never be the same again.

Faith

"O you of little faith, why did you doubt?"
            Matthew 14:31

One of the enduring criticisms levelled at religion is the notion that it requires blind belief: a kind of intellectual surrender. For example:

> *"Religion is about turning untested belief into unshakable truth.."*
> *Richard Dawkins, Author of 'The God Delusion'*

Richard Dawkins is also recorded as saying:

> *"Blind faith can justify anything.."*
> *The Selfish Gene*

Indeed, to many, faith means abandoning reason, closing the eyes, and jumping off a cliff in the hope that something will catch them. My proposition is that this idea is not only mistaken—it is spiritually dangerous, so I happily agree with such criticism.

There is no merit in faith that lacks understanding. In fact, faith without understanding is not faith at all.

Historically, religion has not always helped. Prior to the invention of the printing press, Catholic clergy conducted services in Latin—intelligible only to the learned. The common people, unable to understand what was being said, were kept in a state of manufactured reverence and dependence. Their faith, such as it was, stemmed not from truth, but from ignorance.

Swedenborg writes strongly on this matter:

> "At the present day the term Faith is taken to mean the mere thought that the thing is so because the church so teaches... it is a faith of hearsay... This is not spiritual faith."
>
> Doctrine of Faith 1

Instead, we are meant to understand what we believe. Real faith is not blind trust. It is the rational, internal acknowledgement of truth. It is faith because it is true, not merely because someone in authority said it should be so.

> "Real faith is nothing else than an acknowledgement that the thing is so because it is true."
>
> Doctrine of Faith 2

And importantly:

> "If such a person does not see the truth of a thing, he says, 'I do not know whether this is true, and therefore as yet I do not believe it.'"
>
> ibid.

Faith, then, is not the suspension of reason, but its fulfilment. It begins with an examination of what is true, and then proceeds to believe because we understand. This belief, born of understanding, is what gives rise to true spiritual freedom. Faith frees the will, which is what Jesus said:

> "You shall know the truth, and the truth shall make you free."
>
> John 8:32

And this is the key. Freedom is not found in ignorance. It is found in clarity. In seeing what is good, understanding it, and choosing it. That is faith. And only through this process do we actually become transformed - enlightened.

Swedenborg connects this process directly to the structure of the human mind:

> *"Be it known that charity and faith make a one as do the will and the understanding... charity is of the will, and faith is of the understanding."*
>
> Doctrine of Faith 18

If faith is placed only in the will—without intellectual understanding—it becomes blind emotion or superstition. But if it is seated in the understanding, then it becomes a tool of choice. We see what is good, and freely choose it.

This is where the transformational power of faith lies—not in passive belief, but in the voluntary act of aligning with what is understood to be true. That is what gives rise to regeneration, to the remaking of our inner self.

This is why even a mustard seed of faith has power:

> *"Assuredly, I say to you, if you have faith as a mustard seed... nothing will be impossible for you."*
>
> Matthew 17:20

Not because faith is a magic spell, but because even a tiny seed of understood truth, once believed and acted upon, changes the entire trajectory of one's life.

The David and Goliath story, spiritually understood is another powerful symbol of how living truth (faith) can cast out even the greatest misconception and overwhelming feeling of hopelessness. But, some may ask, can this actually be understood?

Swedenborg makes a profound statement on why spiritual truth can be understood:

> *"The reason spiritual matters are comprehensible is that a person's intellect can be raised into the light of heaven,*

the light in which only spiritual matters are seen, which are the truths of faith."

Doctrine of Faith 3

Faith is therefore a matter of spiritual sight, not spiritual blindness. It is light by which we see what is real—light that reveals both our internal state and the path forward. When people say "I have faith," we should ask, "In what?" And more importantly, "Do you understand why?"

Jesus constantly called His followers not just to believe, but to perceive:

"If you have faith and do not doubt... whatever things you ask in prayer, believing, you will receive."

Matthew 21:21-22

Doubt arises from lack of clarity—not knowing the truth. Faith, in contrast, arises when the understanding is opened and the will is aligned.

We are probably familiar with the term "Amen", which means "It is true", or can be translated as "Truly" or "So be it". Its origins is in the Hebrew and Aramaic pronounced *"āmēn" or "āmīn"* include to be confirmed, to be dependable, to be faithful, to have faith and to believe. It covers all of these.

This tells us something important: faith is not separate from truth. Faith is truth, believed because it is seen and understood. However, understanding alone is not enough. A merely intellectual faith—truth acknowledged but never lived—is hollow. It is faith without essence, like a tree without fruit.

Swedenborg is unequivocal in his book *Doctrine of Faith*:

"Saving faith... is impossible to all except those who are in charity."

Doctrine of Faith 24

> *"Faith separated from charity is no faith, because charity is the life of faith: its soul and its essence."*
>
> *Doctrine of Faith 69*

Faith must be expressed in action. As we will read later, it must be lived in usefulness. This is where the will returns. Understanding shows us what is true. But love—our core affection—must choose it. Only then is the circle complete.

This is the great spiritual mystery: faith only begins in our understanding, but it must return through the will as use. That is what transforms the soul. As Paul says:

> *"But someone will say, "You have faith, and I have works." Show me your faith without your works, and I will show you my faith by my works."*
>
> *James 2:18*

and:

> *"For in Christ Jesus neither circumcision nor uncircumcision avails anything, but faith working through love."*
>
> *Galatians 5:6*

It is then obvious that faith is not irrational. It is not the opposite of logic. It is the culmination of logic illuminated by spiritual light. It is the recognition of truth—understood inwardly and lived outwardly.

Such faith is not blind. It sees with a clarity the natural eye cannot comprehend. It does not ask us to stop thinking, but it demands that we think deeply, seek wisdom, and freely choose what is good. Only then can it be truly said:

> *"This is true, and therefore I believe it."*
>
> *Doctrine of Faith 2*

Truth

"I am the way, the truth, and the life."

John 14:6

*P*eople often speak of truth as if it is something they possess. "I have the truth," they say—be it in politics, religion, or science. However, truth is not something we can ever fully own, but rather something we can align with and strive toward.

Truth is frequently mistaken for perception or belief. What we call true is often just what we want to be true, what fits with our desires or supports our identity. And yet, our desires and our limited intellect do not shape what is real. And here it is: *Truth* is just another word for Reality.

Reality is not altered by belief.

"Truth is not really truth unless it is applied to life."

Doctrine of Life 2

And for example:

"But he who does the truth comes to the light,"

John 3:21

Our minds are finite. We look at reality through a narrow lens, each of us from a different angle. What one sees, another does not. But many still proclaim with boldness, "This is the truth!" The arrogance of claiming we *have* the truth must give way to the humility of realising we only ever *approach* it.

What we perceive may be factual in a given moment, in

a given situation, but facts are circumstantial. Truth, by contrast, is eternal.

Let us consider: we say that water boils at 100°C. This is a natural fact. But it is only true at sea level, under standard pressure. Change the altitude or the pressure, and the "truth" shifts. Does that mean it was never true? No. It was conditionally true—a temporal manifestation of an eternal principle.

This leads us to an important distinction: truth is not fact, though facts may reflect it. Truth is also not belief, although belief can serve as a vehicle to approach it.

Truth on its own is inert. It does not change lives until it is understood and applied. To merely *know* a thing is not enough—it must live in us and so it must be loved.

> *"the truth residing with man must first of all become truth in will and action, ...when truths are translated into action ... truth becomes the good which is called the good of truth. ...able to be joined to the internal man, ...*
> *Action comes first, then the desire for it in the person's will follows."*
>
> Arcana Coelestia 4353

Knowledge without application is like a seed left unplanted. And yet we so often mistake knowledge for truth. We collect facts like trophies, having bookshelves full of them, believing them to bestow wisdom. But wisdom is born when truth is married to love—when understanding meets intention.

This is the red pill moment—the point of no return.

Truth is not always comforting. It is not always convenient. In fact, like the proverbial double-edged sword, it often cuts away our illusions and pierces the self-made armour of our egos.

This is beautifully expressed by Paul:

> "For the word of God is living and powerful, and sharper than any two-edged sword, piercing even to the division of soul and spirit, and of joints and marrow, and is a discerner of the thoughts and intents of the heart."
>
> Hebrews 4:12

Jesus himself said:

> "Do not think that I came to bring peace on earth. I did not come to bring peace but a sword."
>
> Matthew 10:34

To know the truth means shedding comforting illusions. It means choosing the difficult path of seeing oneself—and others—without disguise. It means seeing not only the facts of what happened, but the spiritual quality of why it happened, and what it means.

To choose truth, therefore, is to choose awakening. It is to step away from ignorance—not always toward comfort, but always toward liberation.

As the Bhagavad Gita declares:

> "There is nothing so purifying in this world as knowledge. He who is perfected in yoga finds it in the Self in due time."
>
> Bhagavad Gita 4.38

And yet, the more one seeks truth, the more one realises how much is yet unknown. A person may believe a thing with great sincerity. But sincerity does not make it true. Faith based on false understanding is still false.

This is why Swedenborg wrote:

> "Faith is not faith unless it is the internal acknowledgment of truth."
>
> Doctrine of Faith 2

And so our task is not to possess truth, but to be possessed/transformed by it. Not to argue over who is right, but to seek our own alignment with what is real—what is of the Lord.

The sun does not rise, and the moon does not shine of its own accord. These are appearances. The truth is deeper, beyond the surface. Likewise, the person who believes wrongly is not evil for being wrong—just as a good act can be done poorly, or with good intentions misapplied.

The inner reality matters more than the outer appearance. Truth is ultimately another word for *Reality*, and *Reality* is another word for God.

Swedenborg wrote:

> *"It is the same whether it be said, that God is Good itself and Truth itself, or Love itself and Wisdom itself."*
> *Canons of the New Church*

Therefore, to seek truth is to seek God. To resist truth is to resist Reality itself. Truth is incorruptible: It simply *is*.

It does not care for our feelings. It is unmoved by opinion or consensus. It cannot be manipulated by personal emotion or desire. It is beyond culture, language, or time. Reality can never truly be owned.

What we can have is our perception of truth—refined, filtered and shaped by the loves that move us. If we love what is good, we are drawn to what is true. If we love only ourselves, we shape truth to fit our desire:

> *"The love in the will is the end in view, and in the understanding it seeks and finds causes, through which it may advance to its realisation."*
> *True Christian Religion 658*

Truth is a doorway, not a destination. It is a process,

not a possession. The more we understand, the more we realise how little we know. And yet, this is the beginning of wisdom. For wisdom - as we will see next - is not the fullness of knowledge, but the humility of its application.

And so, the more we love what is good, the clearer truth will become. This is enlightenment.

Wisdom

"But wisdom is justified by all her children."

Luke 7:35

People often equate wisdom with intelligence or education. A person who has read many books, earned degrees, or is articulate in speech is frequently labelled "wise." But consider for a moment that true wisdom is something else entirely. Being knowledgeable is not the same as being wise.

There is, in fact, a wide gulf between knowledge and wisdom. Knowledge consists of facts, data, and information—what is stored in the memory. Wisdom, on the other hand, is the living application of truth from love. It is knowing what is true and good, understanding its use, and choosing to live it. To be wise, one must not simply know the truth—but love it, and act from it. Wisdom is truth applied (to life).

Swedenborg puts it very succinctly:

> *"True intelligence and wisdom are seeing and grasping what is true and good. ... When we are devoted to this faith and are in a life in keeping with it, we enjoy the ability to understand and to be wise."*
>
> Heaven and Hell 351

Let me ask you this:
- Can a person be wise if they know what is good but do not do it?
- Can someone be called wise who stores up truths only to use them for selfish ends?

Clearly not. For wisdom is not merely the possession of truth, but the embodiment of it. This principle—wisdom as truth applied to life—is also echoed in Scripture:

> *"Who is wise and understanding among you? Let him show by good conduct that his works are done in the meekness of wisdom."*
>
> James 3:13

Notice how wisdom is here tied not to knowledge alone, but to action—*"good conduct."* Wisdom reveals itself in how we live, not just in what we say or know.

Swedenborg often explains that our mind consists of two essential faculties: the will (what we love) and the understanding (what we think). Knowledge and intelligence live in the understanding, but they become wisdom only when the will—what we love—gives them life.

In other words, wisdom is not just about thinking clearly—it is about loving rightly. And when we love what is true, the understanding is elevated into wisdom, because when we love what is true we also apply it to our lives. Wisdom is not the height of intellect, but the marriage of love and truth in use.

Thus, the wise person is one who is useful—one who applies truth for the sake of others, not for pride, not for power, not for applause.

This is such a powerful concept. Wisdom is measured not by how much we know, but by how much of the truth we live. In this sense, wisdom is spiritual. It relates to eternal things. It is not just cleverness for navigating the natural world; it is guidance for how we align with the Divine:

> *"Therefore whoever hears these sayings of Mine, and does them, I will liken him to a wise man who built his house on the rock."*
>
> Matthew 7:24

The Lord Himself said a wise person builds on the foundation of action: doing the Word, not just hearing it. Swedenborg echoes this beautifully:

> *"Truths are said to have been imprinted on the life when they become matters of will and consequently of action. As long as they remain fixed solely in the memory, and as long as they are regarded on solely an intellectual level, they have not been imprinted on the life. But as soon as they are accepted with the will they are made part of the life, because willing and consequent action are the real essence of the life of a person."*
>
> *Arcana Coelestia 9386*

In the end, wisdom is not about being right; it is about being aligned. Aligned with reality. Aligned with what is eternal. Aligned with the Divine.

Let me say this: If you want to be wise, then seek not just to understand truth, but to *love* it. And in loving it, live it. To know what is right is good. But to *do* what is right—because it is right and because you love the good it brings—is what makes you wise.

> *"For the reception of love and wisdom in equal measure is the essence of what it is to be an angel, and an angel is an angel therefore according to the union of love and wisdom in him."*
>
> *Divine Love and Wisdom 102*

Good and Evil

> *"Woe to those who call evil good, and good evil; Who put darkness for light, and light for darkness; Who put bitter for sweet, and sweet for bitter!"*
>
> Isaiah 5:20

*I*t is universally accepted to distinguish levels of morality as something being either good or evil. Looking back in history, people commonly tend to historically judge Mother Theresa as good and Adolf Hitler as evil. No doubt their actions appear to have been and thinking about those does indeed make people feel good or bad, but what actually makes something good or evil?

I put it to you that neither the external appearance nor personal feelings about the actions or outcomes makes something good or not.

We will later read in the perspective on Peace that heavenly good is required for it. For now therefore, we are looking at the spiritual quality of Good and by extension its opposite - Evil. Before you trip on the perceived loading of the word evil - it will become clear that the word evil can be just as easily be replaced with the term *selfishness*.

From the book of Matthew:

> *"Either make the tree good and its fruit good, or else make the tree bad and its fruit bad; for a tree is known by its fruit. ... A good man out of the good treasure of his heart brings forth good things, and an evil man out of the evil treasure brings forth evil things."*
>
> Matthew 12:33,35

As will be discussed next in the perspective on Judgement, the quality of the action or person is not determined by the outcome, but by the intention or ultimate purpose. People call something "good" when it feels good or seems nice or kind, but I believe that there is a fundamental distinction between doing what feels good and doing what does good. The answer to what "good" actually is, lies in this area of "doing" good. In other words, where the effect or outcome achieves what *is* good.

Thus it is good to look at the ultimate effect or outcome, rather than the act or process itself, but this still does not explain what good actually is.

Let me ask you:
- do you believe there is such a thing as morality or moral absolute that defines what is good?
- what do you think makes something good, good and something bad, evil?
- On what basis ought we to distinguish between the two, if we cannot simply look at the appearance?
- And, would it be reasonable for us to determine what is good by how we feel about it personally?

Please note down your answers and come back to these later.

Many people do call that which they find pleasing – good and what they do not bad. But simply because it feels good, doesn't mean it is actually good. I think that is pretty much self-evident.

I enjoy a glass of cold beer at times or deep fried fish and chips, but that doesn't make it good for me. Likewise, I find it pleasing when people agree with me, but that doesn't mean it is always good for me. (Unfortunately, many people now seem to need protection and trigger warnings for disagreeable ideas and think - foolishly - being sheltered from intellectual conflict is good.) On another practical level it may become more obvious; giving money to a beggar isn't good if it isn't supporting a good use, as it may – for example – aid in feeding an addiction. We will discuss more on this in the perspective on Charity. So it is critical to understand that feeling good and actual good are two very different things. My feeling about something does not determine the quality of it.

Leaving aside these basic natural examples. I want to turn your focus on objective qualities of good and evil. And I put it to you that there is indeed a moral absolute, just like I believe there is an ultimate reality. I believe that without a purposeful creation, as I touched on in my perspective on Creation, there can be no right or wrong apart from some consensus or personal feeling. In other words, there can be no moral absolute or objective standard on morality to define what is good without life having an intrinsically objective purpose.

With a relative purpose, life would only hold the value we place on it subjectively – individually. This means automatically that there is no objective moral right or wrong and thus no good or evil.

In order for something to be objectively good, it must have meaning and purpose, with a lasting positive effect. It must be constructive, not destructive. Only a permanent order is capable of that. Therefore for something to be objectively good, it must work in harmony with reality according to order as it exists objectively.

We can call this reality God, but it goes by many names that may be equally valid to use. In the end though, the terms God and Good can be used interchangeably as expressed by Jesus:

> *"Why do you call me good? No one is good except God alone."*
>
> Matthew 19:17

I put it to you that a clear distinction between was is

good and evil can be discovered in this interesting quote from Emanuel Swedenborg, where he describes the order of how our life's loves in our inner world affect our thinking in his book *Divine Providence*:

> *"Heavenly love and its affections of good and truth and their consequent perceptions, together with the delights of these affections and their consequent thoughts, may be compared to a tree distinguished for its branches, leaves and fruits. The life's love is the tree, the branches with their leaves are the affections of good and truth with their perceptions, and the fruits are the delights of the affections with their thoughts.*
> *On the other hand, infernal love with its affections of evil and falsity which are lusts, together with the delights of these lusts and their consequent thoughts may be compared to a spider and its surrounding web. The love is the spider, the lusts of evil and falsity with their inner subtleties are the net-like threads nearest the den of the spider; and the delights of these lusts with their crafty devices are the remoter threads, where flies are caught on the wing, entangled and eaten."*
>
> Divine Providence 107, Emanuel Swedenborg

Good, like a tree, is outward looking and seeks to be of use. In fact, perhaps it may be defined as use (or purpose) itself. In a similar way I describe Peace as being Love in practise, let me describe doing good as being the love of use(fullness) in action. Good seeks to support something outside of itself; to seek useful outcomes for usefulness sake, rather than for ulterior motives of personal selfish gain or reward.

Usefulness is ultimately always for the sake of others and contribute to a need or purpose outside of self. Helping others becoming more useful increases their overall potential for good! Thus, good only achieves and supports use.

Therefore good is productive and produces more potential good, which is in essence unlimited.

Giving of what you have is, spiritually speaking, limitless.

Consider a community where all are seeking to serve others in any way they can? There is never a lack of care or support around and everyone would receive as much, if not more, than they give.

- How good would it be to live in such a community?
- Would you call that good or heaven?
- Would you like to live in such a community?

This can indeed be compared to a fruit tree, which produces seed that is capable of producing ever more fruit trees and so forth... This same example can be found in all of nature's reproductive forms.

Therefore only creation, production, use, effort - an objective for selfless reasons - can be good. Good requires a purpose outside of itself. Good therefore requires God. Thus God = Good and Good = God.

> ".. the Lord, who is good itself and truth itself. There is no other source of the love of good and of truth from good"
>
> *True Christian Religion 419*

Abundance and life are the end result of good.

> "Give, and it will be given to you: good measure, pressed down, shaken together, and running over will be put into your bosom. For with the same measure that you use, it will be measured back to you."
>
> *Luke 6:18*

This too (through usefulness or good) is how the spiritual is made constructively manifest in the natural:

> *"the correspondence of natural phenomena with spiritual ones, or of the world with heaven, takes place through use, and that the uses are what unite them."*
>
> Heaven and Hell 112

On the other hand therefore, it's opposite: Evil - like a spider is inward looking and seeks to serve the self only. Evil is only concerned with self and therefore the terms evil and self (or selfishness) can be used synonymously.

Evil seeks to dominate and control others to manipulate outcomes for personal gain. I describe evil as the love of self in action. Because of this it is destructive.

Taking from others, is self-limiting. Consider a community where all are seeking to serve themselves only. Where each is trying to dominate and rule?

- How long do you think this would last?
- How good would it be to live in such a community?

This can indeed be compared with the behaviour of a spider, sitting in its web, trying to take what it can. Perhaps, to use another example, a black hole, as we are told, absorbing and destroying everything around itself and in its path. Or even perhaps, using a scriptural example, the dead sea – with living water flowing in, but nothing flowing out. It is the perfect image of consumption without re-production, destruction and death is the end result.

I hope this gives you a new perspective on *Good* and *Evil* and the timeless battle between these, which we all fight inside our minds. Truly our internal character affects our outer world and each little step to good brings heaven closer to home.

Judgement

"Judge not, that you be not judged. For with what judgment you judge, you will be judged"
Matthew 7:1-2

People tend to place judgement on others most of the time. It is common to blame, to see fault or draw conclusions, simply based on what we hear or what we observe, but I suggest that judging the internal state (or nature) of someone by their external actions is fraught with problems.

Judgement is a key concept in many religious philosophies, but can we legitimately make a value assessment on the spiritual effect of particular actions? Is it a legitimate thing to judge a person?

Well, we may perhaps judge some of the external actions' outcomes as long as we don't transfer the judgement to the inner quality of the person. Actions do not per se tell us anything about the quality of the person's character or the intentions.

The prophet Isaiah gives us a very beautiful passage where it reads:

"And He shall not judge by the sight of His eyes, Nor decide by the hearing of His ears"
Isaiah 11:3

Judging the action or sin is common in the Christian world. You may also be familiar with the phrase "Love the person, but not the sin", but even that is fraught with danger of misconception - judging by hearing or judging by sight - because we must understand the intent in order to know the actual quality of the action itself, and how can we know the intent?

Well the answer really is: "You cannot know the intent, unless the person themselves discloses it to you and makes it known."

Here is another great statement from the spiritual philosophy given to us by Emanuel Swedenborg:

> *"Everyone who has the church present with him is saved; but everyone who does not have it present is condemned."*
>
> New Jerusalem and Its Heavenly Doctrine 245

And in terms of church Swedenborg refers to what is good and what is true, which we will show in more detail in a later chapter! As you can see, the scripture passages that I've just shared with you link the external action such as speech and judgement of others to the heart. This heart factor is a critical attribute for it to be good or evil, and that means that we effectively judge ourselves by developing a specific quality of mind and heart through the choices that we ourselves make. This is because it's the quality of our heart - the quality of our intentions - that determine whether or not our actions are good and thus not the action itself!

Therefore, we are responsible for ourselves. We cannot judge others, but only our own intent, which stems from our core love, and it is this what judges us. Spiritual (inner) transformation therefore takes a lot of sincere introspection and this regeneration process is what determines our ultimate quality and aim.

Now while we talk about judgement, we cannot step around the issue of being saved or the ultimate judgement. Swedenborg writes in Divine Providence:

"...the tree lies where it falls."

Divine Providence 277

and so to our life remains its basic quality when we die. He expresses that we remain who we are when we die. We are all judged according to our deeds. It is not that these are tallied up but that we return to them and behave the same. We return to the same pattern of behaviour based on the quality that is within.

So to conclude, can we legitimately judge others or determine whether their actions are good or not? - we cannot. The inner spiritual quality and aim is what determines the external quality of our lives and our actions. To take it on for ourselves means we can only judge our own intent - not other's, and that stems from our core love, which is effectively what judges us.

We judge ourselves through the choices that we make and how we grow our own inner spiritual character

Forgiveness

"To the Lord our God belong mercy and forgiveness, though we have rebelled against Him."

Daniel 9:9

Forgiveness isn't getting past something by gritting our teeth, nor is it a polite veneer that hides resentment. It's not "forgetting" and it's not merely saying the words "I forgive". These common ideas of what forgiveness actually is misses a deeper more profound approach.

In Scripture and lived discipleship, forgiveness is a letting go — a refusal to let the past prejudge the present or the future. It's the decision to stop carrying yesterday into today. It is an act of freedom, a practice of love, and a way of seeing ourselves and others the way God sees us: not by a running scorecard, but by the heart we hold right now.

Paul highlights this for us:

"Brethren, I do not count myself to have apprehended; but one thing I do, forgetting those things which are behind and reaching forward to those things which are ahead"

Philippians 3:13

Forgiveness is not suppression. Burying anger only plants it deeper in a growing and festering resentment. It is not denial either. Real forgiveness looks wrongdoing in the eye and releases the debt without pretending it never happened. It is not passivity. Sometimes love confronts, sets boundaries, and seeks justice; forgiveness simply means we refuse to nurse the injury into a permanent identity — for them or for us.

Love does not keep an account of a wrong suffered, nor looks at externals. It only looks at the heart - as it is this very moment alone.

> *"For the Lord does not see as man sees; for man looks at the outward appearance, but the Lord looks at the heart."*
> 1 Samuel 16:7

Forgiveness is a letting go of claims on the past. It does not rewrite history, but it refuses to let history rule. The biblical vision is wonderfully concrete: when a person turns, the record no longer defines them:

> *"But if a wicked man turns from all his sins which he has committed, keeps all My statutes, and does what is lawful and right, he shall surely live; he shall not die. None of the transgressions which he has committed shall be remembered against him; because of the righteousness which he has done, he shall live."*
> Ezekiel 18:21-22

This is how God deals with us. The Lord does not stare at old ledgers; he looks at the living heart. The Lord's own posture is the measure and motive for ours:

> *"And be kind to one another, tenderhearted, forgiving one another, even as God in Christ forgave you."*
> Ephesians 4:32

In the New Church theological tradition, Emanuel Swedenborg described what divine forgiveness looks like from heaven's side:

> *"I have heard from heaven that the Lord forgives to everyone his sins, and never takes vengeance nor even imputes sin, because He is love itself and good itself; nevertheless, sins are not thereby washed away, for this can be done only by repentance."*
>
> *True Christian Religion 409*

God's stance is unchanging mercy; what changes is whether we will let that mercy in — by actually letting go of the evils we cling to. So forgiveness is not amnesia; it's transformation.

> *"Sins are not abolished, but removed; and they are removed so far as man continues to refrain from them and enters upon a new life."*
>
> *True Christian Religion 539*

Here are some steps you can use to practise forgiveness:

- Name the wrong without rehearsing it. We speak the truth about what happened — to God, and where wise, to the person — but we do not keep re-reading the wound.
- Release the debt. We deliberately renounce the inner judge that keeps score. This is an act of will, often repeated.
- Seek the other's good (wisely). Love can set boundaries, involve accountability, or even invoke just authority — yet it aims at restoration, not revenge.
- Live from the present heart.

We are told how important this is:

"For if you forgive men their trespasses, your heavenly

Father will also forgive you. But if you do not forgive men their trespasses, neither will your Father forgive your trespasses."

Matthew 6:14-15

And:

"Jesus said to him, 'I do not say to you, up to seven times, but up to seventy times seven.'"

Matthew 18:21-22

And on the cross:

"Father, forgive them, for they do not know what they do."

Luke 23:34

To conclude then, to forgive is to refuse to let the worst moment become someone's final name. It is to regard them by their current character and emerging choices — the way God regards us. When we turn, God does not hold yesterday's transgressions over our head; he meets us where our heart is now.

Forgiveness therefore is a courageous trust in grace. It does not trivialise harm or erase consequences; it simply refuses to be governed by them. Having released the past, we are free to seek a future that looks like Christ and let yesterday's shadows have no rule over today's light.

Prayer

> *"Before they call, I will answer; And while they are still speaking, I will hear."*
>
> Isaiah 65:24

People often think of prayer as words—carefully chosen phrases, set forms, or spontaneous petitions. But I put it to you that prayer, in its essence, is not firstly what we say; it is what we will.

True *Prayer* is a wishing—an interior desire aimed at something. As such, prayer is intimately the same as loving. As we will read further on, our love is our will; and what we most deeply will is what we are forever "saying" to heaven with or without our lips.

> *"for your Father knows the things you have need of before you ask Him."*
>
> Matthew 6:8

Swedenborg is unambiguous about the primacy of the will (love) over mere speech:

> *"The love in the will is the end in view, and in the understanding it seeks and finds causes through which it may advance to its realisation."*
>
> True Christian Religion 658

A person's life is therefore the shape of their love and if love is the end we continually pursue, then prayer—being what we wish for (or will)—is with us constantly. It follows that we are always praying, because we are always willing. This is why Paul is asking us to:

> *"pray without ceasing"*
>
> 1 Thessalonians 5:17

The point is not endless talking, but an unbroken intention toward good. Swedenborg describes prayer on its simplest level as conversation with God that carries an inward view of what we truly desire:

> *"Prayer, considered in itself, is talking with God... and at the same time some inward view of the things which are being prayed for."*
>
> Arcana Coelestia 2535

Note that this prayer includes some "inward view." That inner sight is the will's aim—the love that moves us. Our spoken prayers are good when they express that inner aim truthfully. But when lips say one thing and life seeks another, the words are empty.

The Lord Himself puts it starkly:

> *"These people draw near to Me with their mouth, And honour Me with their lips, But their heart is far from Me."*
>
> Matthew 15:8

If prayer is an outward sign of inward desire, we need not inform the Divine of anything—as if He were unaware. To highlight another beautiful passage on this topic:

> *"For there is not a word on my tongue, but behold, O Lord, You know it altogether."*
>
> Psalm 139:4

The point of prayer is not Divine information, but human re-formation: aligning our will with what is good and our understanding with what is true.

Because what a person loves above all is constantly present in his thoughts (see chapter on *Love*), each of us is continually offering a living prayer—either heavenly or hellish—by what we choose to love. If we love usefulness, truth, and our neighbour, our whole life "says" Your will be done. If we love control, reputation, and indulgence, our life says my will be done. And heaven simply answers the prayer we live.

This is why the Lord urges us to pray "in spirit and truth".

Words help when they express life; but life—the love we habitually choose—is the prayer.

> *"Let the words of my mouth and the meditation of my heart be acceptable"*
>
> *Psalm 19:14*

Love

> *"A new commandment I give to you, that you love one another; as I have loved you, that you also love one another."*
>
> John 13:34

People use the expression love when we like something or someone or when we refer to some kindness or talk about intimately making it, but I put it to you that loving a person is something entirely different.

As you will read in detail throughout this book, Swedenborg tells us that the will is part of the human mind and that the mind is who we are. Our mind is our spirit and thus who we are - the true us - and not our physical body. The human mind has two faculties or two parts: one is the will and the other one is the understanding. Swedenborg uses the Latin word *volentatis* (volition or will), which is also translated as 'choice', 'desire' or 'wish'. This is important, so when Swedenborg uses the terms love, life and will or volition synonymously that is an interesting element for us to then take into consideration.

In True Christian religion we read:

> *"Love itself, and things to do with love, are lodged in the will; knowledge, intelligence and wisdom are lodged in the understanding. The will breathes its love into these"*
>
> True Christian Religion 658

The will then is the being or essence of a person's life.

> "As a result, what one's love and so one's intelligence are like determine what one is like oneself. The will then is the being (esse) or essence of a person's life, but the understanding is the coming-into-being (existere) or arising from this. Since an essence has no reality unless it is endowed with a form, so the will has no reality unless it is in the understanding.
>
> The will therefore takes a form upon itself in the understanding, so that it may come to light. The love in the will is the end in view (aim), and in the understanding it seeks and finds causes through which it may advance to its realisation."
>
> Ibid.

Love is our will and that means it is our essence or our life. In other words it is what animates us and it is what makes us who we are. I don't think there is a better explanation to be found than Swedenborg's description:

> "A person's life is really the same as his love; and what his love is like determines what his life is like, in fact his whole personality. But what makes a person is his dominant or ruling love. ... What belongs to the dominant love is loved above all.
>
> What a person loves above all is constantly present in his thoughts and also in his will, and it makes up his life in the truest sense. For example, anyone who loves wealth above all, whether money or possessions, continually ponders in his mind how to get these; he feels the keenest pleasure when he acquires them, the keenest grief when he loses them. His heart is in them. Anyone who loves himself above all, remembers himself in everything, thinks about himself, talks about himself and acts for his own advantage; for his life is a selfish life.

> *Everyone has as his end in view what he loves above all. This is what he aims at in every detail of his life. His will contains something like a hidden current in a river, which drags and carries him away even when he is doing something else, for it is what motivates (animat = animates) him. This is the kind of thing one person looks for and sees in another, and, depending on what he sees, he either leads him or acts jointly with him.*
>
> *A person's character is determined by the dominant factor in his life, and this is what distinguishes him from other people. This factor makes his heaven, if he is good, his hell if evil. It is his real will, his self and his nature, for it is the real essence of his life. It cannot be changed after death, for it really is the person."*
>
> *New Jerusalem and Its Heavenly Doctrine 54-58*

So what this means is that what we love is what we want to be. It is our ultimate aim. To love then, is to want it to be so. Therefore loving a person is not about being nice or desiring to be or actually being intimate in the bedroom, but it's willing or desiring a person to be. Willing them to exist and to express life freely and happily, which then underpins a totally different perspective on loving a person, on loving oneself or loving the Neighbour.

> *"The universe as a whole and in every detail was created out of divine love, by means of divine wisdom. ...*
>
> *Love without wisdom (or our volition apart from our discernment) cannot think anything. It cannot actually see, feel, or say anything.*
>
> *By the same token, wisdom apart from love (or our discernment apart from our volition) cannot think anything, see or sense anything, or even say anything.*
>
> *If you take the love away, there is no longer any intention, so there is no action."*
>
> *Divine Providence 3*

Peace

> *"Peace I leave with you; My peace I give to you; not as the world gives do I give to you. Do not let your heart be troubled, nor let it be fearful."*
>
> John 14:27

People use the expression peace to refer to the absence of conflict, lack of violence or call something peaceful when the environment is silent or relaxing, but I ask you to consider that true peace means something completely different.

Referring to Emanuel Swedenborg we read:

> *"..heavenly peace flows in when the desires arising from the love of self and the love of the world are taken away. These are what take peace away, for they infest man's interiors.."*
>
> Arcana Coelestia 5662

While, in *Heaven and Hell* - probably his most famous work - he tells us from section 290 onwards:

> *"...on earth they call it peace when wars and conflicts between nations are over, or enmities and disagreements between individuals, ... they think inner peace is simply the peace of mind we have when anxieties are banished, or especially the relief and delight when things turn out well for us. ... this peace of mind, this relief and delight when anxieties are banished and things turn out well for us, may look like effects of peace; but they do not come from real peace except in people who are focused on*

heavenly good. This is because peace occurs only in that good. Peace actually flows in from the Lord into the very core of such individuals, and from that core comes down and spreads into their lower natures, causing peace of mind, relief of the spirit, and a consequent joy."

Heaven and Hell 290

So we can see that is quite a different way of looking at it. He goes on to say that for people engrossed in evil, meaning selfish desires, there is no peace, just an apparent calm or tranquility and pleasure when they get their way, but this is only an external facade, while internally there remains hostility and selfish cravings. In *True Christian Religion* Swedenborg writes:

"...those who enjoy a conscience live in tranquil peace and inward blessedness when they act according to conscience..."

True Christian Religion 666

and elsewhere again:

"Divine Peace is within the Lord, arising from the oneness of his divine nature..."

Heaven and Hell 286

In other words we find that when we act in accordance with our true nature - when there is no dissonance between what we think and how we act - then we have an absence of inner conflict. What we love fundamentally affects our state of mind, it affects our quality of being as a result of that.

Outer conflict, such as war and anxiety et cetera, comes as a result of our inner conflict, which in itself is caused by our selfish actions or selfish desires. So then inner conflict arises when we act in contrast to what we know to be true and or when reality conflicts with our innermost desires.

This means that outer/external peace is only possible as a result of inner peace or inner spiritual harmony with what is good and true - with objective reality - and inner peace in itself then comes only from acting in accordance with our conscience and therefore with what we know to be true.

This is also meant by what we read in scripture in John:

> *"And you shall know the truth and the truth shall set you free."*
>
> John 8:32

It's the absence of conflict and also beautifully depicted by the journey from Egypt to the promised land in the Torah.

We can see therefore that world peace, actual external world peace, is near-impossible: Simply because we cannot eradicate selfishness. Where people are involved, there will be people focusing on themselves.

The best therefore, we can actually hope for and fight for, is to eradicate our own inner selfishness and allow a peaceful state of mind establish itself within us and as a result of that establish peace within our world.

I'll leave you with a beautiful promise:

> *"There are two things at the heart of heaven, innocence and peace.*
>
> Heaven and Hell 285

Charity

"Take heed that you do not do your charitable deeds before men, to be seen by them. Otherwise you have no reward from your Father in heaven."
Matthew 6:1

Most people believe that it is charity to give money to the poor or organisations that coordinate relief efforts to those in need, such as the poor and sick. To some extent that can indeed be charity. But I propose to you that merely giving money to those who have none, or offer salary donations to a charitable institution, is not charity per se and, that for charity to be truly charitable, it must incorporate a key element that is often overlooked.

We previously looked at the spiritual concept of Good, which now leads us into a logical extension of doing good: the concept of *Charity*, as these two are intimately related.

It is universally accepted that it is incumbent upon all humans to look after those who cannot do so for themselves. Like an inbuilt moral radar, we feel we must look after the weak and the vulnerable. It is not a uniquely accepted teaching of Christianity either, where we are called to look after our neighbour for example in the Gospel of Luke:

> *"Then Jesus answered and said: A certain man went down from Jerusalem to Jericho, and fell among thieves, who stripped him of his clothing, wounded him, and departed, leaving him half dead. Now by chance a certain priest came down that road. And when he saw him, he passed by on the other side. Likewise a Levite,*

when he arrived at the place, came and looked, and passed by on the other side. But a certain Samaritan, as he journeyed, came where he was. And when he saw him, he had compassion. So he went to him and bandaged his wounds, pouring on oil and wine; and he set him on his own animal, brought him to an inn, and took care of him. On the next day, when he departed, he took out two denarii, gave them to the innkeeper, and said to him, Take care of him; and whatever more you spend, when I come again, I will repay you. So which of these three do you think was neighbour to him who fell among the thieves?
And he said, he who showed mercy on him. Then Jesus said to him, Go and do likewise."

Luke 10: 30-37

As mentioned, most consider charity to be the giving of food and money, especially to the poor, but many fail to consider the ultimate effect.

I have shared in the chapter on *Good and Evil* that there is a big distinction between doing what feels good and doing that which actually does good. While it may be easy to gloss over, it is actually an important point to grasp. The reason, why I highlight this distinction between doing that which does good and merely doing what feels good, is that a great many simply decide from emotion alone something to be good or not, and so then fail to rationally consider the end-effect.

Let me give you an example, one you will very likely have encountered yourself. Consider a beggar on the street, asking for a couple of dollars for the bus-fare or to pay for some food. Then consider two different approaches:

The first is to simply give what is asked - money. Now, for argument's sake, pretend the person is actually an alcoholic or drug addict, seeking funds to feed his or her addiction.

- Do you believe giving money and thereby feeding or facilitating an addiction is achieving a good end?
- Do you believe you are providing what the person really needs?
- Do you believe giving money in such an instance is actually charitable?

On a side note, much of the money donated to organisations, like government taxes, are spent on bureaucratic administration and wasted on incompetent projects without really helping - or worse, paying sales commissions or bonuses, and after causing unfortunate effects.

Now try another approach - offer and be willing to buy what is ultimately suggested: the bus fare, some shoes or food. You cannot force a bus fare, shoes or food onto the person, and you may simply waste your time and money, but say the person accepts your offer as they truly need to eat and truly haven't the money. Then you have offered something that is beneficial and really needed. Then you have actually done good, haven't you?

This example may be relatively straightforward and makes the point clear enough I hope. This is because the action is most closely associated with what is generally understood already to be charity. But being charitable is an attitude that goes beyond and actually spans all of life's aspects - not just the giving of alms.

It also extends into the realm of justice, politics, family life and work.

A great many people today call for justice, which to them means retribution. Sometimes the more emotional the victim or circumstances, the stronger the penalty called for. Luckily we haven't got the death penalty in Australia, but some countries do.

Charity in justice is not about penalising offenders and satisfying the need for retribution to appease the anger of the community and victim, it should be about the fundamental aspects of restitution and maintaining order.

The aim of our justice system should be to seek to provide a strong enough consequence to prevent criminals from acting in the first place, but also to make sure they understand and learn why they shouldn't do it again - to facilitate a change of heart. Mere punishment doesn't operate from charity, especially if it is driven by anger, but a changed criminal does.

This approach is not dissimilar to how parents interact with their children. Same elsewhere in life. Where rational consideration is given to the ultimate outcomes, where dealings are honest and genuine, where priority is laid with the result, rather than the perception, that is where we find charity at work.

To sum it up, let me make a few points.

So my first point then is to suggest to you that charity is not generosity in itself. It is not the blind offering of money, food or clothing to the poor. It is not simply the giving of fish.. so to speak. It goes beyond that.

I suggest to you that true charity is doing what does good. In other words: doing (what does) good is charity. It is aiming to achieve a good outcome, regardless of what is looks like. It requires rational consideration to what is really needed and what the ultimate outcome is that may be achieved.

In his work *Charity*, Emanuel Swedenborg writes the following about charity requiring prudence:

> *"Whoever does not distinguish the neighbour according to the quality of good and truth in him may be deceived a thousand times, and his charity become confused and at length no charity. A man devil may exclaim, "I am a neighbour: do good to me." And if you do good to him he may kill you or others. You are placing a knife or a sword in his hand."*

> *Charity 51*

> *"Genuine charity itself is prudent and wise. Other charity is spurious, because it is of the will or of good alone, and not at the same time of the understanding or of truth."*
>
> Charity 54

Of course, it doesn't have to be as dramatic as to facilitate murder, the negative effects can be much more subtle or not even involve an external victim, as I highlighted before.

My second point is that true charity requires us to be personally committed - emotionally - in wanting to achieve a good outcome. (see also next chapter on *The Neighbour*) To wish well and to do actual good, regardless of our own recognition in the process. In other words, that it is only charitable if we prioritise the usefulness or good it achieves and not take our own merit into consideration. There is nothing charitable about patting yourself on the back, telling yourself how good you are.

> *"But when you do a charitable deed, do not let your left hand know what your right hand is doing"*
>
> Matthew 6:3

Swedenborg uses the term evil, but selfishness can be used synonymously, where he explains that we ought to remove our own self-interest and meritorious views:

> *"To will to do good to the neighbour is of charity. This is known, for it is believed that to give to the poor, to assist the needy, and many other things, are goods of charity. But yet they are goods only so far as the man shuns evils as sins. If a man does them before he shuns evils as sins they are external goods, yea, done for the sake of merit. For they flow forth from an impure*

fountain; and the things which issue from such a fountain are inwardly evils. The man is in them, and the world is in them."

Charity 17

"It is clear then, from these considerations, that the first of charity is to shun evils as sins; which is done by repentance. Who does not see that an impenitent man is evil? And who does not see that an evil man has not charity? And who does not see that he who has not charity cannot do charity? Charity must be from charity within a man."

Charity 11

Now as I highlighted in my previous chapter on *Good and Evil*, Good requires a moral absolute (ie an objective purpose to reality). It requires a use outside of itself and thus good can only be selfless. In other words, good does not exist in a state of selfish desire. This is what we just read in Swedenborg too.

Swedenborg equates charity with doing good and he focuses on the neighbour as good itself. Meaning, that doing good can only be good when it is for the sake of achieving good and that this aim is the neighbour in spiritual terms.

In Paul's writings we have a beautiful example in Tabitha:

"This woman was full of good works and charitable deeds which she did."

Acts 9:36

It comes then as no surprise that in order to be charitable and do good, one must understand what good actually is. That someone who seeks good fears inadvertently achieving a bad outcome, which may be best illustrated by this final passage from Swedenborg.

> "Not to will to do evil to the neighbour is of charity. Everyone sees that charity does no evil to the neighbour; for charity is love towards the neighbour, and he who loves anyone fears to do evil to him. There is a conjunction of souls between them. Whence it is that when one does evil to him to whom he is conjoined by love, he has a perception in his soul as if he were doing evil to himself. Who can do evil to his children, to his wife, to his friends? For to do evil is against the good of love."
>
> Charity 14

I hope this then makes it clear that true charity is to express our love for good usefully - doing what does good.

The Neighbour

"You shall love your neighbor as yourself."

Mark 12:31

All Christians know they are asked to love the neighbour and so try to be kind to others, especially those nearby—family, friends, colleagues, or the less fortunate. Indeed, many point to the words of Christ as evidence for this all-encompassing love:

> *"But I say to you, love your enemies, bless those who curse you, do good to those who hate you…"*
>
> *Matthew 5:44*

From this, some conclude that loving the neighbour means to offer unconditional affection or acceptance to all, regardless of their behaviour.

And while this seems admirable, consider that loving the neighbour is not merely about being agreeable, tolerant, or loving humanity as a whole. Building on the chapter on *Charity*, let us explore what it truly means to love the neighbour: the object of charity. Swedenborg writes:

> *"to love the neighbor does not mean loving a companion in respect to his person, but loving the truth that is from the Word; and to love truth is to will and do it."*
>
> *Heaven and Hell 15*

This is a significant, but an essential distinction.

To love the neighbour therefore, is not to affirm all people equally, nor to condone all behaviours, but it is to will the good that is in another, and to support what is good and true in them—what is of the Lord.

That which is destructive, selfish, or false is *not* the neighbour and is *not* to be loved (ie not to be 'willed'). In fact, to support what is evil in someone is not love at all, for it ultimately harms both them and the community.

This false version of "love" is often what the world offers: a tolerance of all behaviour, even if it corrupts, but the Lord teaches otherwise:

> *"You have heard that it was said, 'You shall love your neighbor and hate your enemy.' But I say to you, love your enemies, bless those who curse you, do good to those who hate you, and pray for those who spitefully use you and persecute you, that you may be sons of your Father in heaven; for He makes His sun rise on the evil and on the good, and sends rain on the just and on the unjust. For if you love those who love you, what reward have you? Do not even the tax collectors do the same? And if you greet your brethren only, what do you do more than others? Do not even the tax collectors do so? Therefore you shall be perfect, just as your Father in heaven is perfect."*
>
> Matthew 5:43-48

Swedenborg explains that the neighbour is not a static category of people, like the poor, or our countrymen, or even our enemies, although we certainly have a civic duty to those people. Instead, "the neighbour" increases in quality as the good in a person increases:

> *"The neighbour is to be loved according to the quality of good in him... the neighbour is the good itself which is to be loved in a person."*
>
> Charity 38

So when we are told to love our neighbour, we are being asked to love that which is of the Lord in another person. To will what is good and true for them—not simply to show them affection or approval.

And what is it that is of the Lord?

"I am the way, the truth, and the life."

John 14:6

To love the neighbour is to love the truth and goodness that flow from the Lord. This is what binds communities together in heavenly order. This is what Swedenborg also calls *uses*, or functions, beneficial to others. In contrast, to support, or excuse what is selfish, deceitful, or harmful is to act against the neighbour. Loving the neighbour can only be through supporting what supports their eternal welfare!

Humanity

"Then God said, 'Let Us make man in Our image, according to Our likeness...'"

Genesis 1:26

People commonly equate being *human* with our species —*homo sapiens sapiens*—biological creatures capable of intelligence, empathy, language, and social cooperation. We speak of human rights, humanitarian aid, or of someone being humane, suggesting compassion and care. But I believe that this understanding of humanity is superficial at best and falls short of what it truly means to be human.

Let me start by suggesting something radical: we are not human because we are biologically of the species *homo sapiens*. We are human only inasmuch as we receive and reflect what is truly human—that is, what is *Divine*.

In the original languages of the Scriptures, the word for "man"—*Adam*—is not a reference to maleness or even necessarily a person. *Adam* is a word that means *mind* or *thinking being*, and it is only through this capacity that we are distinguished from the animal kingdom.

Emanuel Swedenborg makes it explicitly clear:

"It is through the understanding that a human being is a human, and is distinguished from a beast."

Divine Love and Wisdom 240

And:

"It is the human mind, and this only, that distinguishes a person from the beasts; and the human mind is

> *distinguished into two faculties, which are called the will and the understanding."*
>
> Divine Providence 73

These faculties—the will and the understanding—are the very image and likeness of God in us. When we speak of becoming "human," then, it is not something we are by default, but something we become by aligning these faculties with Divine Love (the will) and Divine Wisdom (the understanding). Only then do we reflect the image of the Divine and become truly human.

If we are honest, mere biology cannot account for our inner life—our capacity to reflect, to yearn for justice, to contemplate eternity, or to weep at beauty. We sense within us something more, something *not* of the dust. Our body may be the vessel, but our spirit—the mind—is the actual person.

> *"Whoever duly considers the subject can see that as the body is material it is not the body that thinks, but the soul, which is spiritual."*
>
> Heaven and Hell 432

In the Bhagavad Gita, Krishna affirms a similar truth:

> *"Weapons cannot cut it, fire cannot burn it, water cannot wet it, wind cannot dry it. This self cannot be destroyed."*
>
> Bhagavad Gita 2:23-24

In Matthew we read:

> *"do not fear those who kill the body but cannot kill the soul. But rather fear Him who is able to destroy both soul and body in hell."*
>
> Matthew 10:28

So while the body may perish, the mind—the soul—is eternal and capable of union with the Divine. But that union is not automatic. It depends on our receptivity—our willingness to *receive* what is truly human: love, truth, and usefulness.

Jesus tells us:

> *"Abide in Me, and I in you. As the branch cannot bear fruit of itself… neither can you, unless you abide in Me."*
> John 15:4

Here the Lord identifies Himself as the *vine*, and we the *branches*. In other words, our humanity is only real when connected to the source of all that is truly human. Outside of Him, we are not human in the highest sense—we are merely sensual.

Swedenborg writes:

> *"Let nobody suppose that anyone is man because he has a human face and a human body, and has a brain and also organs and limbs. All of these he has in common with animals, and therefore these are the things which die and become a corpse. But a person is man by virtue of his being able to think and will as a human being, and so of his being able to receive things that are Divine, that is which are the Lord's."*
> Arcana Coelestia 4219

This is not to say we are worthless or evil without religion or spiritual knowledge. Rather, it is to recognise that our true humanity is measured by our capacity and willingness to receive what is higher—what is divine—and to live from it.

We read in Genesis that we are created in God's image. This image is not physical—God is not flesh and blood—but the image of love and wisdom. As we act from love and according to wisdom, we manifest what it means to be made in God's image.

Therefore, our humanity is not found in our capacity to reason, but in *how* we reason. Not in our emotions, but in *what* we choose to love. Not in our ability to act, but in *why* we act. These are what determine whether our spirit (our mind) is aligned with the Divine Human—Jesus Christ.

As Swedenborg so beautifully writes:

> *"For the Lord alone is Man, and angels and spirits, as well as people on earth, are likewise men only insofar as they are dependent on Him."*
>
> Ibid.

When we act from self, live for self, and trust in self alone, we fall from humanity. We devolve. Not biologically, but spiritually. We no longer receive from the Divine, and so we begin to perish inwardly. Like a branch broken off from the vine, we wither.

The Qur'an too warns:

> *"Have you seen the one who takes as his god his own desire?"*
>
> Qur'an 45:23

Such a person no longer reflects the Divine but merely the impulses of the ego. True humanity is lost when we live only for self—because self alone is finite, limited, and perishable.

So what does it mean to truly become human?

It means to allow our mind—our spirit—to be aligned with what is eternal. To think not just about ourselves, but about others. To act not just from impulse, but from conscience. To love not what flatters the ego, but what is useful, good, and true.

Humanity is not an accident of evolution. It is a Divine

calling. We are only truly human when we *receive* what is human from its Source: the Lord, who is Love itself and Wisdom itself. As Paul wrote:

> *"You are not your own... therefore glorify God in your body and in your spirit, which are God's."*
> 1 Corinthians 6:19-20

Let us then aspire to be human. Not by form, but by spirit. Not by inheritance, but by reception. In this way, we fulfil our name—*Adam*—the thinking being, the spirit that reflects the Divine.

Spirituality

"It is the Spirit who gives life; the flesh profits nothing. The words that I speak to you are spirit, and they are life."

John 6:63

It is common to use the term spirituality to refer to activities such as meditation, yoga, fortune-telling, praying, going to church or just being religious. Others think that it is about finding stillness or self affirmation, and or perhaps even seeking to fulfil their deepest internal desires, but I put it to you that true spirituality is none of these and something different.

Let me start by asking you a few questions:
- Do you believe spirituality is an activity or that engaging in a particular activity makes one more spiritual? For example yoga or meditation?
- Do you believe being spiritual is seeking to become holy, enlightened or wise?
- Do you consider a drive to fulfil your innermost desires by various activities to be spirituality?

To me spirituality and being a spiritual person has little to do with any particular activity, but everything to do with the attitude and mindset we bring to the activities we perform.

Having to do with the spirit, we must first accept we have a spirit, which Swedenborg also describes as our mind - the conscious part of us that is our actual identity. If we are to be spiritual, we must recognise and accept that there is a meta-physical reality (ie "spiritual world") and that this unseen reality is intrinsically connected with us right now.

We also need to accept that this spiritual reality is ruled or guided by specific spiritual qualities, such as good and truth or love and wisdom and that our efforts here have an effect on our spirit and have therefore long-term consequences - as already discussed in previous chapters.

Let us have a look at some scriptural references and quotes:

> *"God is Spirit, and those who worship Him must worship in spirit and truth."*
>
> *John 4:24*

> *"The kingdom of God does not come with observation; ... the kingdom of God is within you."*
>
> *Luke 17:20-21*

Swedenborg tells us that our feelings and thoughts (and thus our spirit) are not in space and time and that we can be intimately present with others in feeling and thought. This then means that thinking from the perspective of space and time has nothing to do with spirituality and being spiritual, but thinking from what is infinite and eternal or real does.

> *"The reason angels and spirits have such powers of being present is that every affection of love and so every thought of the understanding is non-spatially in space and non-temporally in time."*
>
> *True Christian Religion 64*

> *"Space and time have nothing to do with this presence, because a feeling and its consequent thought are not in space and time, and spirits and angels are feelings and their consequent thoughts."*
>
> *Divine Providence 50*

And further...

> *"This leads us to the conclusion that we should think about what is infinite and eternal and therefore about the Lord non-temporally and non-spatially,"*
>
> Divine Providence 51

Therefore, spirituality is not an activity, but an active principle of loving good and truth in your life and affirming this as being due to what is infinite and eternal. (In other words outside of space and time)

Being a spiritual person therefore, is not the result of an activity you perform, but a state of mind. It is being constantly mindful of the quality that underpins our actions and seeking to affirm and embrace what is real and eternal - the source of all that is good and true. It is therefore looking outside of ourselves for how we can contribute towards effecting good: such as being useful, loving and truthful. By affirming and owning what is good and true, we will attain enlightenment, peace and freedom, even though these personal outcomes ought not to be our primary objective.

Spiritual Growth

"And the little Child grew, and became strong in Spirit, filled full with wisdom; and the grace of God was upon Him."
Luke 2:40

By extension many people think spiritual growth is about mastering stillness or perfecting a discipline like meditation. Others believe it is found through accumulating spiritual knowledge.

But, being spiritual has nothing to do with time and space activities or sense-based thinking. Spiritual growth is not about becoming better at something, but about transforming our spirit (ie mind).

> *"He who overcomes, I will make him a pillar in the temple of My God, and he shall go out no more. I will write on him the name of My God and the name of the city of My God, the New Jerusalem, which comes down out of heaven from My God. And I will write on him My new name."*
> Revelation 3:12

In other words, it is about becoming someone else entirely—someone new. Not someone different from who you are, but growing more fully into the you you are meant to be. This change is not sudden or gifted in an instant, but it is a process of willing transformation, a rebirth of the inner self through the progressive and voluntary application of truth. (ie enlightenment) Let us explore what that means.

True spiritual growth is not found in escaping the

world, in being still, but in engaging with it through a new lens. It is not the practice of withdrawing from life's circumstances, but of learning how to *live through them* with wisdom and love.

Swedenborg tells us that our spirit is our mind, composed of two faculties: the will (what we love) and the understanding (what we think). Spiritual growth occurs when we align our understanding with truth from the love of truth, and then make this living by applying it in use—that is, in real service to others.

It is about aligning our heart to accept what is good and our head to accept what is true.

> *"A person is reformed by means of truths, and by a life according to them."*
> *New Jerusalem and Its Heavenly Doctrine 28*

We are not transformed by knowledge alone, but by what we *do* with it. This doing must spring from love—because what we love is what moves us. Growth, then, is a cycle: truth informs love, love motivates action, and action reshapes us into more spiritual beings.

Swedenborg frequently distinguishes between the *natural* mind and the *spiritual* mind. The natural mind is focused on appearances, on the world of sensation, time and space. It judges success by external gain, pleasure, or reputation. But the spiritual mind begins to see *beyond* appearances—to the causes, the purposes, the divine reality beneath the surface of things.

For those who are merely naturally minded do not see anything from a spiritual point of view, but only from a natural one.

> *"The natural mind which is a hell stands in complete opposition to the spiritual mind, which is a heaven. When loves are opposed, then perception and everything*

connected with it becomes opposed."
Divine Love and Wisdom 276

To grow spiritually is to begin this inward movement—from sense to spirit, from self to service, from ego to essence. It is not abandoning the world, but learning to navigate it rightly. To live in time while thinking from eternity.

This is what Paul refers to when he writes:

> *"And do not be conformed to this world, but be transformed by the renewing of your mind, that you may prove what is that good and acceptable and perfect will of God."*
>
> *Romans 12:2*

One may ask: why do so many remain spiritually stagnant? Because truth is often acquired for the sake of pride, identity, or power. But such truth does not transform. Only truth that is loved: truth sought *and lived* because it is true and useful, enters into our being and becomes a part of who we are.

> *"Enlightenment comes only from the Lord, and to those who love truths because they are true, and make them their guide to a useful life. No others find enlightenment in the Word. ...*
>
> *The reason only those are enlightened who love truths because they are true, and make them a guide to a useful life, is that they are in the Lord and the Lord is in them; for the Lord is truth itself, as was shown in the chapter on the Lord."*
>
> *True Christian Religion 231*

When truth is loved, it challenges us. It confronts our lower loves and demands their reordering. It brings discomfort, because growth always does. But if we submit to it—if we use truth as a mirror for honest self-examination and a guide for constructive change—we are gradually remade. In this process too, we become more clearly our own true selves.

Spiritual growth, though, is not linear. It is not a staircase upward, but a spiral. We revisit old struggles with new light. We stumble, then stand again. This is what Swedenborg calls *regeneration* the life-long process of being spiritually reborn.

> *"In man's regeneration however the Lord draws out every single thing in its proper order, separating them all from one another and arranging them so that they may be turned in the direction of truths and goods and may be joined to them. And this takes place varyingly according to people's states, which are countless as well."*
>
> *Arcana Coelestia 675*

We are not growing toward some vague enlightenment, but into ever deeper states of harmony with reality—with Divine order. We are growing into people who no longer live for self, but for what is real and eternal: the good of others, the truth of the Lord, and the joy of usefulness.

> *"And we all, with unveiled face, beholding the glory of the Lord, are being transformed into the same image from glory to glory..."*
>
> *2 Corinthians 3:18*

Therefore, Spiritual growth is not about mastering techniques, but about becoming a vessel for the Lord's love and wisdom. It is about loving what is true, choosing what is good, and living usefully. It is a movement from external appearance to internal substance, from the sensual to the spiritual.

Christianity

"By this all will know that you are My disciples, if you have love for one another."
John 13:35

Most people think of a Christian as someone who believes in Jesus Christ, reads the Bible—especially the New Testament—and goes to church. Some say you must be baptised to be Christian, while others argue that only those within their own religious denomination are truly saved. Whole sects claim exclusive ownership over the path to heaven, over who qualifies as *Christian* and who does not.

But I suggest to you that Christianity is not defined by labels, buildings, or rituals!

A true Christian is someone who follows the Lord Jesus Christ—knowingly or unknowingly—by loving what is good, and living according to what is true, and seeking to be of use in their life. One who acknowledges and lives by Reality itself, which is Goodness and Truth, follows the Lord regardless of religious affiliation or self-ascribed identity.

As we read in the Gospel of Matthew:

"Not everyone who says to Me, 'Lord, Lord,' shall enter the kingdom of heaven, but he who does the will of My Father in heaven."
Matthew 7:21

This might seem uncomfortable to some, but this perspective aligns with what is revealed in the internal sense of the Word. The Lord is not confined to a title or a specific body of believers. The Lord is Goodness itself and Truth itself. So, whoever submits to a higher power, sincerely seeks what is good, lives according to truth, and strives to be useful to others, is in the Lord—even if they've never read a single verse of scripture.

Swedenborg reveals that:

"The Word is the Divine truth itself... and the Lord is the Word."

True Christian Religion 3

This means the Lord is not just the man born in Bethlehem, but the Divine Human—the fullness of Love and Wisdom. To follow Him is not just to call on His name with our lips, but to live by what He *is*—to will what is good, to understand what is true, and to act from these in the service of others. That is Christianity in its most essential form.

Those who act from conscience and a sincere love of what is right, even if they have never heard the name Jesus, are closer to Him than those who claim to know Him but live contrary to His spirit. In fact, the more a person resists selfishness and seeks usefulness to others, the more the Lord is present in their life.

This is echoed in Swedenborg's *Heaven and Hell*:

"Heaven is not granted from mere faith or confession, but from the life one has lived; and the life that leads to heaven is a life of love and service."

Heaven and Hell 535

This is made very clear by Jesus:

"Whoever does the will of My Father in heaven is My brother and sister and mother."

Matthew 12:50

And again, in His sobering warning:

> *"Anyone who speaks a word against the Son of Man, it will be forgiven him; but whoever speaks against the Holy Spirit, it will not be forgiven him."*
> Matthew 12:32

This is often misunderstood. But seen in the light of Swedenborgian insight, the Holy Spirit represents living truth actively proceeding from the Lord—the reality of what is good and true. To speak against this—to knowingly reject what is right and true, previously accepted, in favour of selfish falsity—is to cut oneself off from salvation. It is not about not knowing the historical Jesus, but about rejecting Goodness and Truth themselves.

This then is the essence of Christianity.

The term *Christian* originates from the Greek *Christos*, which means "Anointed One", and historically was applied to those who followed the teachings of Jesus. Yet, obvious as it may now seem, this external title does not guarantee internal transformation.

> *"Faith is nothing unless it is a life of love to the Lord and charity toward the neighbour."*
> Arcana Coelestia 2228

Christianity cannot be a mere creed or confession, nor about church membership or attendance. It is about becoming a new person—someone who lives for the sake of others, who acknowledges a Divine Source outside themselves, and who progressively seeks to unite the will to love with the understanding of truth in life.

The Divine is always present, always seeking to restore order by embodying (think re-birthing) what is good and true, wherever and however that may be received.

It follows then, that there are many invisible Christians in the world—those who do not identify with the term, but who live the life of true Christianity. They love others, seek truth, and live in service to others. Their lives are Christian in essence, if not in name.

Conversely, there may be many who bear the name, but who live contrary to its spirit.

> *"Why do you call Me, 'Lord, Lord,' and do not do what I say?"*
>
> *Luke 6:46*

The core message is this: Christianity is not about affiliation—it is about transformation. To be Christian is to embody Christ—not in (external) name, but in life.

By now it will be completely clear that The Divine is Goodness and Truth itself. Jesus Christ is the embodiment of that in Human form—Reality itself. Therefore, all who sincerely love the good, live by what is true, and acknowledge the existence of a Higher Source, are connected to Him.

It is not mere knowledge of the Lord that saves, but conformity to Him in life. Those who serve others in love, and who act from truth and integrity, are truly His followers.

Let us not limit Christianity to the visible signs and symbols. Instead, let us recognise the Christian life wherever love is expressed through truth for the sake of others.

That, I put to you, is True Christianity.

Spiritual Christianity

"But the natural man does not receive the things of the Spirit of God, for they are foolishness to him; nor can he know them, because they are spiritually discerned."
1 Corinthians 2:14

*P*eople often label things "spiritual" to give them credibility or deeper meaning—spiritual music, spiritual practices, spiritual wisdom. But simply calling something spiritual doesn't make it so. Nor does calling something Christian automatically mean it reflects the true spirit of Christianity.

The same is true in reverse: just because something doesn't look traditionally "Christian" doesn't mean it isn't. For at the heart of Christianity is not the external appearance, but the inward life—how we live from the Spirit and according to spiritual principles.

Let us take a moment to distinguish between what might be called religious Christianity and what I would describe as *Spiritual Christianity*. Religious Christianity is often bound by doctrine, ritual, tradition, and external observance. Spiritual Christianity, on the other hand, is grounded in life—the inner transformation of heart and mind through loving what is good and understanding what is true.

In *True Christianity*, Emanuel Swedenborg writes:

"The church is not where the Word is, nor where the Lord is named, but where people live according to the Word and love the Lord by doing His commandments."
True Christian Religion 510

This means that being Christian—truly Christian—is not simply about profession, affiliation, or belief, but about spiritual life. That is, truth applied to life. As has been said before: wisdom is truth applied to life, and spirituality is nothing if not lived.

The chapters on both *Spirituality* and *Christianity* have laid the groundwork for this understanding. Spirituality, we saw, is not an activity but a state of mind—a heart that seeks what is infinite and eternal. And Christianity, we saw, is not merely about naming Jesus but embodying His principles of goodness and truth.

So what is *Spiritual Christianity*? It is, quite simply, the living out of divine truths in daily life. It is Christianity stripped of ego and pride, without the need to be "right" or to judge others. It is the way of humility, usefulness, and transformation.

Spiritual Christianity, therefore, is not founded on dogma, but on divine order. It is the inner church—*the Lord's presence in the will to do good and the understanding of truth.* It is what this book is grounded in.

Even though the theological framework of this book draws deeply from the spiritual philosophy of Emanuel Swedenborg—perhaps the most comprehensive spiritual revelation ever —these perspectives are not about defending a doctrine, but about highlighting *principles.* Timeless spiritual laws. Living truths. What is useful, eternal, and true.

As Scripture itself reminds us:

"God is Spirit, and those who worship Him must worship in spirit and truth."

John 4:24

Spiritual Christianity is love in action. Not love as a feeling, but love as a will to do good. And not truth as a collection of facts, but truth as light that guides that love in wise and useful ways.

It's time we return to the root of what Christianity was always meant to be—a way of life rooted in the Spirit of the Lord, who is Divine Love and Divine Wisdom.

And in this, there is ultimate freedom:

> *"Where the Spirit of the Lord is, there is liberty."*
> *2 Corinthians 3:17*

The Church

"on this rock I will build My church"

Matthew 16:18

Many people today believe church to be a building. Some think of it as a Sunday ritual in a dedicated hall or cathedral. Others may associate it with a religious organisation, a denomination, or even a spiritual community.

For most, Church is a place where people gather to pray, sing songs, and hear sermons. But I like you to believe that Church is none of these things in and of themselves, and that its true nature is something completely different.

As by now you may begin to see, let me suggest instead that Church is the presence of the Lord in a person's life. More specifically: Church exists wherever the Lord is received.

This may seem like a strange statement, especially if you've grown up believing that only certain people, structures, or rites have spiritual legitimacy. But let us look deeper. In *Heaven and Hell*, Emanuel Swedenborg writes:

> *"The church is the Lord's heaven on earth, and the individual is a church when he is in good and truth from the Lord."*
>
> Heaven and Hell 57

This means that Church is not a fixed place, nor an organisation, but something inward—something spiritual. It is not something we go to, but it is something we become. Where the Lord is received—that is, where love and truth are acknowledged and lived—there is Church.

This is exactly what the Lord Himself says:

> *"For where two or three are gathered together in My name, I am there in the midst of them."*
> Matthew 18:20

So, what does it mean to "gather in His name"? Is it about saying "Jesus" aloud or posting scriptures on the wall? No. It is about embodying in our lives what His name represents.

> *"The Gentiles shall see your righteousness, And all kings your glory. You shall be called by a new name, which the mouth of the Lord will name."*
> Isaiah 62:2

Spiritually speaking, one's name is one's character or quality. In the Lord's case: Goodness and Truth. When two or three people come together genuinely seeking what is good and true, and submitting to it, not just in word, but in will and deed, then the Lord is present—and therefore, so is the Church.

When Swedenborg speaks of 'the church', he does not mean a particular institution. Rather, he refers to the presence of good and truth in a person's life.

> *"Everyone who has the church present with him is saved."*
> New Jerusalem and Its Heavenly Doctrine 245

This 'church' is internal—it is one's love of what is good and one's living by what is true. So the true church is scattered throughout the world, across cultures and religions, wherever people love their neighbour and live sincerely.

> *"The church is where the Word is and where the Lord is known by means of it."*
>
> True Christian Religion 246

Again, this is not referring to the physical book itself, nor the reciting of its verses as ritual, but rather the living Word—the divine truth received and applied.

Just as Heaven is not a location in space but a state of being (as discussed earlier), so too is Church a state of reception. It is where heaven begins—because it is the soil where seeds of heavenly life are planted.

> *"The kingdom of God does not come with observation; nor will they say, 'See here!' or 'See there!' For indeed, the kingdom of God is within you."*
>
> Luke 17:20-21

Church, then, is not defined by visible rituals or walls but by *invisible reception*. If you live your life grounded in what is good and true—if you welcome the Divine Love and Wisdom into your inner being—you are a Church - the Lord's dwelling place. You are heaven in miniature.

This is why someone who never steps foot inside a formal church building may be more *of the Church* than someone who attends weekly but lives selfishly. True Church is not about attending services, but living in service.

This aligns beautifully with the words of Jesus:

> *"But the hour is coming, and now is, when the true worshipers will worship the Father in spirit and truth; for the Father is seeking such to worship Him. God is Spirit, and those who worship Him must worship in spirit and truth."*
>
> John 4:23-24

Buildings may honour God, but it is the inner temple

of the heart that determines one's true belonging. And if Church is the Lord's dwelling, then it is a moving, breathing, living thing—wherever His spirit is welcomed.

This is not to say that physical church gatherings are without use. On the contrary, when done sincerely, they can be powerful vehicles for spiritual growth and fellowship. But they are not the essence. The essence is reception—and that can happen anywhere, even in the solitude of your room or the quiet integrity of your choices.

In this way, the concept of Church brings us full circle: it is heaven's outpost on earth. And heaven, as we have said, is not somewhere we go, but a way of being. So too, church is not something we attend, but something we become. And thus, Church is not confined to any one place or people. It is within reach of every heart, open to what is real.

Freedom

"where the Spirit of the Lord is, there is liberty"
2 Cor. 3:17

*F*reedom is often understood as the power or ability to do whatever one pleases—free from rules, constraints, or consequences. This idea is especially seductive in youth, where rebellion against imposed authority is often equated with liberty.

However, I suggest to you that this concept of freedom is not only shallow, but ultimately self-defeating. If freedom means doing what we want without consideration or consequence, it fails to acknowledge a fundamental truth: *every thought, every word, every action has an effect*. Here too Swedenborg sums it up perfectly:

> *"For every smallest fraction of a moment of a person's life entails a chain of consequences extending into eternity. Indeed every one is like a new beginning to those that follow,"*
>
> *Arcana Coelestia 3854*

In other words, there are no isolated actions. Everything is connected, and our choices always ripple into our own lives and into the lives of others. This is a spiritual law just as immutable as gravity is a natural one.

Epictetus the Greek Stoic Philosopher is quoted as saying:

> *"a man is not free who is not master of himself."*
>
> *Epictetus (50-135AD)*

How true this is. What good is it to be able to follow our desires if we are slaves to them? What kind of freedom is it, if we are tossed around by every emotion, every impulse, every reactive thought without awareness or control?

The Lord's commandments are often perceived as limitations, or worse, as burdens. Yet what if they are in fact descriptions of reality? What if they are not arbitrary rules, but invitations to live in alignment with how things actually are?

When we resist the nature of reality, friction arises. And when we align with it—when we live in truth, in goodness, in love—there is harmony. In other words, the less we fight reality, the freer we become to express the highest loves of our heart.

Swedenborg provides a profound insight into this dynamic. He explains that the human mind consists of two faculties: the will and the understanding.

True freedom, then, is not found in the will alone—because our desires can be twisted, selfish, or short-sighted—but in the harmony between the will and the understanding.

When we know what is good and true, and we choose it from love, we are truly free. Not living in harmony with reality is tantamount to living in a fantasy - at some point you must wake up and face the consequence of reality, which may be much more than mere disappointment.

> *"Angelic freedom consists in being led by the Lord, and infernal freedom consists in being led by oneself. The latter appears as freedom, but is slavery; while the former appears as slavery, but is freedom."*
>
> Heaven and Hell 598

True freedom is the ability to act in accordance with our deepest loves *from* a position of wisdom. It is not the shallow liberty of choosing without knowledge, but the profound liberty of *knowing* what is real and choosing it freely. This kind of freedom requires that we are aware of the consequences of our actions—not because we fear punishment, but because we understand our participation in the whole.

> "You shall know the truth, and the truth shall make you free."
>
> John 8:32

In this sense, truth is not merely information. Truth is reality. And true freedom is the unlimited ability to live in accord with it. The more we know of what is good, and the more we choose that good from love, the more we are liberated and feel to be more clearly our own selves—not free from responsibility, but free from internal conflict and contradiction. We are no longer torn between competing selves or desires. We become one: whole, true, and free.

The Bhagavad Gita captures a similar sentiment, describing the person who is truly liberated as one who is not entangled in the fruits of action, but who acts from clarity and love:

> "Those who perform prescribed duties without desiring the results of their actions are actual sanyāsīs (renunciates) and yogis."
>
> Bhagavad Gita 6:1

Freedom is not exemption from law—it is living in harmony with it. And as Swedenborg reminds us, Divine laws are not imposed from without, but arise from the very structure of reality itself: love and wisdom are the foundation of all things.

> "The essence of God is Divine Love and Divine Wisdom,

and these two make the very life which is God."
Divine Love and Wisdom 14

When we live in alignment with these—when we act from a love of what is good, guided by wisdom of what is true—we are free indeed. Not because we can do anything, but because we *choose* what is right. This is the freedom to become our true selves.

Let me close by summarising:
- Without truth, there is no wisdom.
- Without wisdom, love becomes blind and erratic.
- Without choice, there is no freedom.
- But without *wise* choice—freely chosen—there is no *true* freedom.

True freedom is therefore the freedom to choose reality —*to act from love, in truth, for the sake of good*: acting from an enlightened will! Anything less is illusion. Anything more is Divine.

Male and Female

> *"So God created man in His own image; in the image of God He created him; male and female He created them."*
>
> *Genesis 1:27*

People often think of male and female as merely biological categories—genetic differences resulting in varying body parts or hormonal balances. Some would argue it's all a result of random chance in the evolutionary lottery. But I propose that the male and female sexes are not simply variants of human anatomy or mere social constructs (the lunacy!). Rather, as all things have their cause in the spiritual, the physical form too reflects a deeper spiritual reality. It is not biology that makes gender —it is the spirit.

Emanuel Swedenborg teaches that everything in the natural world exists because of something spiritual that precedes (ie causes) it. This includes gender. In *Divine Love and Wisdom*, he writes:

> *"the spiritual world is here first..., for all causes are there; and... the natural world, where all things... are effects."*
>
> *Divine Love and Wisdom 119*

This means the distinction of male and female is not just skin deep. It is the result of a spiritual principle manifesting itself into the natural world. But here lies the paradox: The Divine itself is neither male nor female—and yet both exist within it. The Lord is not divided. He is perfect love and perfect wisdom—Good and Truth united.

In this, we glimpse the Divine Marriage: the eternal

union of Love and Wisdom within the Divine, which flows into creation in a myriad of ways—including the human form.

Note the wording in Genesis: "in the image of God... male and female." Both are equally expressions of the Divine image, but they do not mirror (or correspond to) it in the same way. Instead, they each embody a different aspect of that image.

According to Swedenborg, the masculine originates in its love for wisdom—or said differently, in the desire to give effect to, and so do what is good, through Truth. This is why The Word manifests as male. This shows up in men as a stronger predisposition for logic, facts and understanding - ahead of, and sometimes even separated from, emotion.

The feminine, on the other hand, originates in a love for that Truth in action —a love for wisdom as the expression for Good. To say it differently, the feminine embodies the love for doing good. This is why the Divine reception in Mary was needed to conceive the Word. This shows up in women as a nurturing to ensure good is effected and a stronger disposition for the affectionate - ahead of, and sometimes even separated from, logic, facts and understanding.

These are not just abstract ideas. They are profound realities that show up in the ways men and women think, feel, and relate to one another. The are complimentary and infilling to make each other more complete.

> *"The male is born to become understanding and the female to become will for the sake of the understanding. Thus, the male is truth and the female is the affection for that truth."*
>
> Conjugial Love 32

That is to say: a spiritual man seeks truth and from understanding then desires to do good, while a spiritual woman carries the love for affecting good and then desires the wisdom to achieve it.

Swedenborg puts it like this:

> *"man is born to be intellectual, that is, to think from the understanding, while woman is born to be affectional, that is, to think from her will"*
>
> Heaven and Hell 368

I like to express it as saying that the feminine infills the masculine with the love for good, while the masculine gives effect to this love. This complementarity, though often misunderstood in the natural world, is at the heart of spiritual union. When these two aspects unite—not just physically, but mentally and spiritually—they mirror the Divine Marriage. This is why it is said:

> *"The two shall become one flesh."*
>
> Genesis 2:24

Swedenborg explains this spiritual oneness:

> *"In marriage love, each partner sees the essence of themselves in the other. There is a mutual and reciprocal union of souls and minds, and thus a conjunction of the inner self."*
>
> Conjugial Love 180

This is not mere romance. This is a profound metaphysical truth: that true male and true female form a union that transcends individuality and forms a complete human in the image of God. Neither alone is complete. Each is a part.

And that is the point. We are not the Divine—we are its image, and so we are limited. And it is through mutual love, truth, and wisdom that we may each begin to complete our human form in spirit.

The Apostle Paul echoes this mystery when he says:

> *"Nevertheless, in the Lord woman is not independent of man, nor is man independent of woman."*
> 1 Corinthians 11:11

True masculinity and femininity are not opposites, but counterparts—co-creators in the spiritual journey of becoming. The union of male and female is a call not merely to partnership in the natural world, but to participate in the Divine pattern. A pattern where love flows into wisdom, and wisdom returns to love—creating life, order, and joy.

It is also important to say this: every individual—regardless of sex—has both faculties within them. Swedenborg affirms that the mind consists of both will (love) and understanding (truth) in all of us, so the purpose of spiritual development is to harmonise both within ourselves too. Just as the Divine is One, we are to become more whole. Growing individually and conjointly.

So then, male and female are not mere biological functions, but windows into the very nature of the Divine. And when they unite in spiritual love, they form something far greater than the sum of their parts—a living representation of heaven itself.

As Swedenborg puts it:

> *"Married love is the fundamental of all loves in heaven."*
> Heaven and Hell 366

Marriage

> *"For in the resurrection they neither marry nor are given in marriage, but are like angels of God in heaven."*
>
> Matthew 22:30

Most people tend to think of marriage as a formal contract between two people—sometimes as a religious sacrament, other times merely as a social institution or legal agreement. Some see it as a convenience for sharing finances, raising children, or gaining societal approval. But I put it to you that marriage is none of these things in its essence.

Marriage, in its truest and deepest sense, is not a contract, but a conjunction of minds: a spiritual union between two people, flowing from the Divine. It is not founded on law or custom or passion alone, but on the harmonious unity of two inner lives, each reflecting and receiving the other in love and wisdom.

Swedenborg calls this spiritual union conjugial love, and it is unlike any other form of love. He writes:

> *"marriage is the completion of a person, for by marriage a person becomes a complete person"*
>
> Conjugial Love 156

This love is not found in mere romantic feelings or mutual attraction, which can exist even in people who do not truly know one another. Nor does it arise from compatibility of taste or personality, but from a spiritual likeness in pursuit of a shared life in truth and goodness.

Each spouse serves as the other's complement,

forming a single complete spiritual being.

In the previous chapter, we saw that the masculine originates in truth from good, while the feminine originates in love for that truth. When these two unite—each from its own nature and in mutual respect—a third emerges: a shared life that is neither his nor hers, but theirs. A new wholeness. A new heaven. Here is another beautiful passage from Swedenborg:

> *"Male and female were created to be the very image of the marriage between good and truth. This is because the male was created to be an expression of the understanding of truth, thus a picture of truth, and the female was created to be an expression of the will of good, thus a picture of good, and implanted in both from their inmost beings is an inclination to conjunction into one. Thus the two together form a single image."*
>
> Conjugial Love 100

This is why marriage is more than physical intimacy, more than friendship, and more than cohabitation. It is the living out of Divine order in the human form:

> *"The origins of conjugial love are internal and external, there being many internal origins, likewise many external ones. The inmost or fundamental origin of them all, however, is one. This is the marriage between good and truth."*
>
> Conjugial Love 83

To put it simply: real marriage is Divine order in expression.

This helps explain why so many marriages in the world are unfulfilling or even destructive. The external form may exist—a wedding, a shared home, legal documentation—but the internal union is missing. The minds are not joined. The aims are separate. The loves are misaligned.

This well known passage is often quoted:

> *"They are no longer two, but one flesh. Therefore what God has joined together, let not man separate."*
>
> Matthew 19:6

It is not about forcefully keeping unhappy couples together. It is about what God joins—not what the state certifies or people arrange for their own ends. What God joins is spiritual. When two people genuinely love the good and truth in one another, when they are joined in use and mutual striving for what is eternal, they become one mind in two forms.

Emanuel Swedenborg again describes it beautifully:

> *"Married partners become proportionately one person in the measure that their conjugial love grows. And because, in heaven, this love is genuine, owing to the celestial and spiritual life of the angels, therefore two married partners there are called two when they are referred to as husband and wife, but one when they are referred to as angels."*
>
> Conjugial Love 177

Marriage is therefore a spiritual pathway. Not everyone walks it, and not everyone who marries in the external sense experiences it. But for those who do, it is a refining fire: it burns away selfishness, calls forth forgiveness, challenges us to become better than we are.

It can be difficult, yet it is holy. Why? Because it works toward mutual regeneration—the spiritual transformation of both individuals into a shared vessel of the Divine.

It is important to say here that true marriage continues after death. The physical body falls away, but the spirit—being the real person—remains. And so does the spiritual union if it was real. Marriage is eternal when it is real. It survives time and outlasts our natural death, because it is not based on the perishable. It is rooted in the Lord.

Some may feel sorrow reading this—perhaps having never known such a marriage, or having experienced brokenness instead. But there is hope.

Swedenborg teaches that conjugial love is available to all who love truth and good, and that in the spiritual world, the right partner may be found even if one was never married on earth. He writes:

> *"in the case of people who after preparation are introduced into heaven, marriage is provided with a partner whose soul inclines to union with the soul of the other, to the point that they do not wish to lead two lives but one. That is why, after separation, a man is given a suitable wife, and a woman, likewise, a suitable husband."*
>
> Conjugial Love 50

This is a beautiful truth and a great comfort. The Lord provides for those who walk in His ways. What we long for in spirit, we are not denied in eternity.

So let me conclude with this: Marriage is not a mere agreement or cohabitation. It is a union of minds and lives, grounded in the Lord and shaped by the complementary truths of love and wisdom. It is an image of heaven on earth. And when truly lived, it is the closest we may come to embodying the Divine Marriage itself.

> *"Everyone, whether man or woman, possesses understanding and will; but with the man the understanding predominates, and with the woman the will predominates, and the character is determined by that which predominates. Yet in heavenly marriages there is no predominance; for the will of the wife is also the*

husband's will, and the understanding of the husband is also the wife's understanding, since each loves to will and to think like the other, that is mutually and reciprocally. Thus are they conjoined into one.

This conjunction is actual conjunction, for the will of the wife enters into the understanding of the husband, and the understanding of the husband into the will of the wife, and this especially when they look into one another's faces; for, as has been repeatedly said above, there is in the heavens a sharing of thoughts and affections, more especially with husband and wife, because they reciprocally love each other.
This makes clear what the conjunction of minds is that makes marriage and produces marriage love in the heavens, namely, that one wishes what is his own to be the others, and this reciprocally."

Heaven and Hell 369

Heaven and Hell

"besides all this, between us and you there is a great gulf fixed, so that those who want to pass from here to you cannot, nor can those from there pass to us."
Luke 16:26

Most people imagine *Heaven* and *Hell* to be physical locations—like a cloud-filled paradise above or physical resurrection here on earth, and a fiery dungeon below. Some imagine pearly gates and harps or devils and pitchforks. While others to the contrary think these are mere fables and imaginary concepts.

But I suggest to you that Heaven and Hell are neither physical places nor imaginary fables at all, but actual *states of being*—states of mind and heart that reflect, and lets us experience, our inner spiritual quality. I dedicate a whole chapter in my book *Divine Healing* on our environment manifesting as a reflection of our internal and I recommend you reading it.

In his book *Heaven and Hell*, Emanuel Swedenborg also makes this abundantly clear:

"Heaven is not outside anyone; it is within. It is found in a person's inner life, in their ruling love."
Heaven and Hell 33

This is possibly one of the most revolutionary insights Swedenborg offers. It flips the conventional picture of salvation and damnation on its head. Instead of being about where we go to after death, Heaven and Hell are about *what we become*—who we truly are in our intentions, our desires, and our loves.

As Jesus unambiguously told us:

> *"the kingdom of God is within you."*
>
> Luke 17:21

It should be clear by now that our mind is our spirit, and our spirit is who we are. Therefore, our mental and emotional state—the quality of our love—*is* our spiritual state. And that determines whether we experience Heaven or Hell, both in this life and in the next.

> *"Hence, on death, everyone goes the way of his love, the man in a good love to heaven, and the man in an evil love to hell, nor does he rest except in that society where his ruling love is."*
>
> Divine Providence 319

This is key. The afterlife is not about judgement in the traditional sense, but about *attraction*. Like attracts like. People gather with others who love the same things—whether those things are selfish and destructive, or generous and useful.

The implication is profound. Heaven and Hell are not given to us after death, based on belief or confession, but rather, they are outcomes of who we have become - the destiny of our ruling love. A selfish person would not be happy in heaven. A loving and generous person would find hell unbearable. We gravitate to our spiritual homes according to the law of attraction: *like attracts like*.

This spiritual law is universal. It governs not only the afterlife but also our experience here on earth. In fact, it is THE LAW, so fundamental that The Lord said that this one rule captures everything: a Golden Rule, which we will discuss in a bit more detail further on.

Why? Because it captures our spiritual will and so

character, which immutably determines our relationship to others and so our spiritual home. We don't need to wait until we pass into the spirit world, we see this play out in daily life already: positive, kind people attract similar souls. Toxic, angry people gravitate toward each other. We are attracted to people, ideas, and environments that resonate with our inner nature. This is not a punishment or a reward, but simply a spiritual reality.

This law of attraction is described clearly in the Qur'an as well:

> *"Indeed, Allah will not change the condition of a people until they change what is in themselves."*
>
> Qur'an 13:11

And in the Bhagavad Gita:

> *"Rajas is born of desire and attachment... it binds the soul through longing. Tamas is born of ignorance... it binds the soul through delusion."*
>
> Bhagavad Gita 14:7–8

What we cling to inwardly determines our spiritual state and path. What we love rules our life. That ruling love gathers around it everything that confirms and feeds it. Heaven and Hell begin within us—right now.

Perhaps the most important thing to understand from this is that no one is *sent* to Hell: people voluntarily go where they feel at home. If a person has lived their life loving only themselves and despising others, they would find the atmosphere of Heaven unbearable. The light would hurt their eyes and the joy of others would be too offensive.

> *"spirits who are absorbed in evil resist strenuously and virtually tear themselves away from the Lord. They are drawn by their evil ... because of their love of evil, ...*

they freely cast themselves into hell."

Heaven and Hell 548

This underscores the immense freedom we are given: we shape our eternity by our present choices. Our daily decisions, the thoughts we entertain, the loves we cultivate —all of these form our spirit. It is as if we each carry within us the seed of our eternal home. Heaven or Hell is not imposed from without. It grows from within.

Clearly then, Heaven and Hell are not places we are, or can be, sent to. They are realities we choose for ourselves. They are states of love. States of mind. They are *what we become,* based on the quality of our intentions and affections. Our choices matter. They shape our spirit. And our spirit is who we are.

Heaven is the love of what is good, true, and useful. Hell is the love of self, control, and gratification. Every thought, every act of kindness or selfishness, shapes us toward one or the other.

So the question isn't "Will I go to Heaven?" but, "Am I becoming Heaven?"

> *"Our love is our life. Whatever our love is like, that is what our life is like — in fact, that is what our whole self is like. But our primary or controlling love is what makes us the person we are."*
>
> New Jerusalem and Its Heavenly Doctrine 54

Let us take a minute to consider then what it means to live in Heaven or in Hell:

Heaven (the love of being useful)

So what does Heaven look like? It is not a reward we are given, but a state we become. And in Heaven, everything revolves around *usefulness*. Everyone seeks to serve others, to contribute to the common good. This brings deep joy, peace, and fulfillment.

> *"All in heaven are associated according to the loves of their lives, which are loves of usefulness; and all the joy of heaven flows from being useful."*
>
> Heaven and Hell 403

Heaven, therefore, is not about idleness or rest in a literal sense. It is about *engaged love*—love in action, love expressed through service and care. The more we love what is good, the more heavenly we become, and the more joy we experience.

People there do not seek recognition or reward. They find heaven in usefulness itself.

> *"For where your treasure is, there your heart will be also."*
>
> Matthew 6:21

This inner orientation shapes not only one's daily thoughts but the entire quality of spiritual life. A person whose treasure is love of good and truth—who delights in doing good for its own sake—is already beginning to live in Heaven.

Imagine a community where everyone lives to help others, not for personal gain, but because they genuinely love to be of service. Wouldn't that be Heaven?

Hell (the love of self)

Hell, by contrast, is also not a punishment inflicted by God! It is the inevitable result of a life oriented inwardly toward self. In Hell, everyone is trying to rule, control, manipulate and take. There is no joy in service—only bitterness when one doesn't get their way. In Hell, each person seeks to control and dominate others. Everyone wants to be served, and no one wishes to serve, except themselves.

Swedenborg explains that in hell everyone is keen to dominate others. When all want this, they come into conflict and mutual hatred. (sound a little like the antagonism between politicians or lawyers, doesn't it?) and that this causes them to experience the inherent torment as a consequence.

> *"since rebellious movements are always arising (everyone there wants to be greatest and burns with hatred against everyone else, which keeps generating new attacks), the scene is constantly changing. The people who were enslaved are released and offer their support to some new devil for the subjugation of others. Then the ones who do not surrender and yield their obedience are tortured in various ways, and so on and so on."*
>
> Heaven and Hell 574

Hell is not about fire and brimstone—it is about *disorder*.

It is the torment that comes from selfishness, greed, and envy. It is a mental state, not just a location. And tragically, people choose it freely—because they love what they love, even if it hurts them. Such people would find Heaven unbearable. The joy of others would offend them. The light of Heaven—a light of love, peace, and innocence—would be blinding. Their own nature would reject it. And so they choose what aligns with their ruling love, even if it is hellish. This was echoed even in the teachings of Paul:

> *"For to be carnally minded is death, but to be spiritually minded is life and peace."*
>
> Romans 8:6

This is a sobering truth: after death, we are not punished arbitrarily, but simply live according to what we have chosen to become.

Innocence

> *" I am pure, without transgression; I am innocent, and there is no iniquity in me."*
>
> *Job 33:9*

*W*hen we hear the word innocence, we may think of a courtroom verdict—"found innocent"—as though innocence is merely the absence of wrongdoing. Others equate it with naivety or ignorance: a child unaware of evil, or someone "too innocent to know better."

But I believe that *Innocence* is neither ignorance nor inaction, nor is it simply a lack of guilt. Rather, true innocence is a spiritual quality of the highest order—an active love of what is good and true, grounded either in simplicity or, even more powerfully, in wisdom.

Emanuel Swedenborg tells us that innocence is loving the Lord above all things and loving one's neighbour as oneself. It is a willingness to be led by Him and not by oneself.

> *"That is why they say in heaven that innocence dwells in wisdom and why angels have as much wisdom as they do innocence. They support the truth of this by observing that people in a state of innocence do not take credit for anything good, but ascribe and attribute everything to the Lord.*
>
> *They want to be led by him and not by themselves, they love everything that is good and delight in everything that is true because they know and perceive that loving what is good - that is, intending and doing good - is loving the Lord, and loving what is true is loving their*

neighbor."

Heaven and Hell 278

At its core, innocence is not the absence of selfish affections (evil) and fallibility, but the presence of good. It is a state of heart—of willing what is good and true, and desiring no harm to another. It is also a state of mind—recognising that all good is from the Lord and choosing to be led by Him rather than our own self-derived understanding.

This innocence is beautiful and pure, but it doesn't start there. In his work *Arcana Coelestia*, Swedenborg explains that:

> *"There is an innocence of ignorance, such as exists with infants and children; and there is an innocence of wisdom, such as exists with the angels. The innocence of infants and children is external and not internal, whereas the innocence of the angels is internal. The one goes along with ignorance, the other with wisdom."*
>
> *Arcana Coelestia 9301*

In other words, the innocence of ignorance is passive and natural—it doesn't yet know how to choose good consciously. The innocence of wisdom, however, is deeply spiritual. It knows both good and evil, and still chooses good —not from fear, not from ignorance, but from love.

This is innocence in its truest, most powerful form: innocence as love in action, enlightened by wisdom.

This may sound contradictory—how can innocence coexist with wisdom? Doesn't knowledge of evil destroy innocence? On the contrary. Knowing evil without loving it is the very foundation of wisdom. A person who has come to understand evil—its causes, its consequences, its deceitfulness—and chooses to turn away from it, is far more innocent than one who simply has never been exposed to it.

> *"Behold, I send you out as sheep in the midst of wolves. Therefore be wise as serpents and harmless as doves."*
> *Matthew 10:16*

This is the nature of the innocence called the innocence of wisdom. For this reason, innocence in adulthood is far more noble than that of childhood, because it is a conscious return to the Lord, as Jesus taught:

> *"Unless you are converted and become as little children, you will by no means enter the kingdom of heaven."*
> *Matthew 18:3*

And again:

> *"Blessed are the pure in heart, for they shall see God."*
> *Matthew 5:8*

It is not childishness the Lord requires, but child-likeness: a state of trust, humility, and openness to submit to reality and being led by the Divine. Innocence is therefore inseparable from humility. In Swedenborg's terms, it is the acknowledgment that nothing good is from ourselves, but all from the Lord.

It is no coincidence that, according to Swedenborg, the highest heavens, where love reigns completely, are filled with those in a state of deepest innocence. The more wise they are, the more innocent they become.

For with true wisdom comes the realisation that all truth and goodness flow from the Divine alone.

> *"There are two things at the heart of heaven: innocence and peace."*
> *Heaven and Hell 285*

Peace and innocence are intertwined because the truly

innocent soul does not resist the Lord. There is no internal conflict - only harmony, because the will is aligned with divine order. Such a soul is at peace, not because they have avoided life's trials, but because they have surrendered to what is truly good. In other words innocence is wisdom clothed in humility. This is why the greatest innocence is also the greatest strength.

The Bhagavad Gita, in its own way, touches on this idea when Krishna says:

"The one who has conquered the mind, who is serene, who sees the same in heat and cold, in pleasure and pain, and in honour and dishonour, is fit for immortality."
Bhagavad Gita 6:7

The truly innocent, then, are not fragile or naive—they are serene and unshakable, because their desires are aligned with eternal realities.

And so, we return to our opening thought: innocence is not about the absence of wrongdoing or a declaration of legal purity. It is not naivety or ignorance. Rather, true innocence is the active desire not to harm, the love of truth, the will to do what is good—not because of external reward or fear of punishment, but because it is good in itself.

In this light, even our judgements of others begin to soften and melt away. The innocent person struggles to attribute evil to another. Not because they deny its existence, but because they see beyond it to the deeper potential within. They see as the Lord sees:

"He shall not judge by the sight of His eyes, Nor decide by the hearing of His ears; But with righteousness He shall judge the poor."
Isaiah 11:3-4

May we all move, then, from the innocence of ignorance

to the innocence of wisdom. From being unaware of good, to choosing it. From avoiding evil unknowingly, to turning away from it deliberately. In this journey, we draw nearer to the Lord Himself, who *is* Innocence incarnate.

> *"innocence constitutes that essentially human quality; indeed innocence is so to speak the basic attribute into which love and charity from the Lord can enter. When a person is being regenerated and becoming wise the innocence of infancy which has been external becomes internal. Consequently true wisdom resides in no other abode than innocence; also, no one can enter heaven except one who has some degree of innocence, according to the Lord's words in Matthew 18:3."*
>
> *Arcana Coelestia 4797*

New Perspectives

Happiness

"Happy is he who does not condemn himself in what he approves."
Romans 14:22

People often talk about happiness as if it were a fleeting emotional state — a warm bath, a good meal, a holiday, or the excitement of achieving something we've long desired. Many believe happiness comes from the outside: from a good relationship, a pay rise, an unexpected compliment, or even a piece of chocolate cake. These things can indeed spark joy, but I put it to you that they are not happiness itself.

True *Happiness* is something deeper — a quiet contentment and inner peace that comes not from getting what we want, but from being who we are meant to be. Not from owning or controlling, but from being useful in the present moment. Not from pursuing selfish desire, but from participating in the order of the universe — that is, from being of service. True happiness is intimately tied to deep sense of fulfilment and the deep peace that exists when we can trust in the Lord and do not feel compelled by a need to control every single moment.

A famous self-help guru once said:

"Happiness is a natural state, you already own it."
Anthony Robbins

In other words, happiness is not something to be gained; it is something to be uncovered. And what hides it is not lack of external pleasure, but internal disorder — when our loves are misaligned.

We read before that a person's life is really the same as his love, and that what we love above all else draws every aspect of our thought and will into service to it. If our love is selfish — for example, love of wealth, control, or reputation — then even when we 'get our way', we are only temporarily satisfied. But if our dominant love is for truth, goodness, and usefulness — if we will the good of others and act in accord with it — then this love brings a lasting inner joy, because, with its unlimited potential, it is in harmony with the Divine.

In his work *Heaven and Hell*, Swedenborg explains about those in innocence (ie heavenly good):

> *"Peace actually flows in from the Lord into the very core of such individuals, and from that core comes down and spreads into their lower natures, causing peace of mind, relief of the spirit, and a consequent joy."*
>
> Heaven and Hell 290

This is what happiness truly is: not the thrill of gratification, but the joy of spiritual peace, the fulfilment of acting from love into usefulness.

We are told by the world around us to believe that happiness is found in "having it all", but let's consider:

> *"How hard it is for those who have riches to enter the kingdom of God!"*
>
> Luke 18:24

Worldly gain, including knowing much, though it can offer comfort and convenience, cannot offer true joy. When we seek to be happy by controlling what is outside us — by demanding that people or circumstances satisfy our personal expectations — we are always set up for disappointment. Our happiness is fragile, easily disturbed by things beyond our control.

Happiness

In contrast we read:

> "Happy is he who has the God of Jacob for his help, Whose hope is in the Lord his God."
>
> *Psalm 146:5*

While those with the gains of evil, who are caught up in the loves of self and the world, according to Swedenborg:

> "may experience apparent calm, tranquillity, and pleasure when they get their way, but this is outward only... inside there is raging hostility"
>
> *Heaven and Hell §290*

This is why what looks like happiness — indulgence, victory, seduction, luxury — often ends in sorrow, exhaustion, and emptiness. This, too, is why approaching spirituality as something to do or to be used as external mask of thin veneer - when we are actually selfish - above our true inner character doesn't bring true and lasting peace and happiness.

True happiness cannot be chased; it must be inhabited. It requires changing our inner nature itself. It exists only in the present moment and only in the act of usefulness. We are never truly happy when focused on what was or what might be — only when we are engaged in something meaningful now.

This is what I believe Jesus means, when He says:

> "Come to Me, all you who labour and are heavy laden, and I will give you rest."
>
> *Matthew 11:28*

The rest being referred to is not idleness, but spiritual rest — that is, inner contentment from living in divine order. We find it when we are acting in accordance with our conscience and fulfilling a useful role in life. Not because we are praised, or because we feel successful, but because we are serving something greater than ourselves. Because we left behind any internal conflict that otherwise exists between knowing what is right and wanting what is not.

Swedenborg echoes this in *True Christian Religion*:

> *"Those who enjoy a conscience live in tranquil peace and inward blessedness when they act according to conscience..."*
>
> *True Christian Religion 666*

Usefulness is **the** key to happiness. When we stop worrying about what we can get or consume, and instead focus on how we can serve — how we can give, contribute, build, support, heal, teach, or simply be present — we begin to experience real joy. Unlimited too, because this opportunity presents itself without limit.

To phrase it differently: The way we frame our inner world determines our happiness. If we focus on what is missing, what is unfair, or what might go wrong, we invite anxiety and discontent.

> *"Which of you by worrying can add one cubit to his stature?"*
>
> *Matthew 6:27*

And again:

> *"Be anxious for nothing, but in everything by prayer and supplication, with thanksgiving, let your requests be known to God."*
>
> *Philippians 4:6*

Swedenborg describes heaven as a state of inner harmony, and all heavenly joy as flowing from the Lord into those who love what is good. In this sense, heaven — and thus happiness — is not something to wait for after death, but something to cultivate here and now.

To do this, we must:
- Change our focus — from lack to gratitude. (get rid of the would've, should've and could'ves!)
- Ask better questions — What can I give? What is the use?
- Soften our rules — Let go of rigid expectations about what "should" happen.
- Stop judging and start perceiving — Learn to see the truth behind appearances.

Freedom from anxiety, bitterness, and discontent begins with aligning ourselves with truth — not our desires or fears, but what actually is. (see John 8:32)

In conclusion: Happiness is not pleasure. It is not ease. It is not constant cheerfulness. Rather, it is the deep joy of being who we are truly meant to be — vessels of love and wisdom, fulfilling our unique place in the web of usefulness that is reality.

It is not about feeling good all the time. It is about doing what is good, and feeling the joy that arises when our inner and outer life are aligned.

As the Lord said:

"Peace I leave with you, My peace I give to you... not as the world gives do I give to you."
John 14:27

That peace is the heart of happiness. And it is not something to find — but something to live.

The Golden Rule

"Whatever you want men to do to you, do also to them."
Matthew 7:12

Most people are familiar with what is known as the "Golden Rule" (quote above). On the surface, this seems to echo a call for kindness and is often interpreted as give in order to receive, but it is much more profound than that. If I truly want what is good and true for myself—eternal life, peace of spirit, and alignment with reality—then I must also will those same things for others - in everything!

The Golden Rule is not a way to get something—it's a way to become something.

The true essence of the Golden Rule is found in its interior quality: it is about willing good for another for their sake, from an understanding that they, like you, are a vessel of the Divine.

Swedenborg explains that true love is not affection alone, but the desire that another be—that they flourish, live, and become more fully human. Loving others is to will the good of another. This is no superficial kindness, but an expression of the very nature of God.

When we say, *"Do unto others,"* the point is not to manipulate outcomes or mimic ideal behaviours in hope of receiving them. The point is to allow the interior principle of love to manifest in our treatment of others. In this way, the Golden Rule is not about imitation—it is about transformation.

Not indulgence. Not avoidance of conflict. But real good.

True love, then, is not permissiveness. It is willing

that others come into alignment with the truth and into usefulness—into *who they really are*, which is found only in connection with the Divine.

Let me ask you a question:
- Is it loving to support someone's destructive behaviour, to ignore a lie, or enable a person's addiction, simply to avoid discomfort?

Of course not!

We recognise that doing so ultimately contributes to that person's downfall. Real love, real neighbourliness, is to support that which uplifts, heals, and restores. That which is useful—not just personally beneficial, but communally beneficial.

Swedenborg writes:

"The quality of the neighbour with a man is in accordance with the quality of the good [and truth] with him; or such as a man is, such a neighbour is he."

Charity 50

As we read before our neighbour is not merely the person next to us or a stranger in need, but is to be seen as the good that dwells within another—their openness to what is true and useful. To love the neighbour is to love the Divine in them; not to tolerate or excuse their evils, but to seek their highest good.

That means the "neighbour" in us is our own will for good, and the neighbour in others is their desire to live in truth and usefulness. To love the neighbour is to affirm this in ourselves and in others. It is to participate in the Divine order. It is not unconditional acceptance, but the unconditional willing of good.

It is a grave misunderstanding to equate Divine love with passive tolerance. In fact, Divine love is fiercely active. It wills to save, to transform, and to make whole. That is why it confronts what is false. That is why it corrects. That is why it *chastens*.

> *"For whom the Lord loves He corrects, just as a father the son in whom he delights."*
>
> *Proverbs 3:12*

So too should our love for the neighbour be willing to challenge, when needed, not for the sake of superiority, but for the sake of what is good.

In conclusion then, to love the neighbour is to love what is of the Lord in another—what is true, what is good, what is useful. It is to affirm the eternal spirit and will the person's alignment with heaven. To love the neighbour is to resist what is destructive and selfish, not embrace it. It is to call people into usefulness, not comfort them in disorder.

Loving the neighbour is loving what is real in them. It is loving the Lord within them and affirming that which supports their eternal welfare. The Lord is the neighbour in the highest sense, and from Him the neighbour originates.

> *"Truth is the neighbour in so far as it makes one with good, and it makes one with it as a form makes one with its essence."*
>
> *Charity 67*

In spiritual circles, the Law of Attraction is often invoked as the principle that "like attracts like." What we project into the world, energetically and spiritually, tends to return to us, and manifests, in some form. This is not magical thinking—it is a spiritual law grounded in correspondence.

We've learned now that Swedenborg reinforces this principle through his teaching on the afterlife: our eternal spiritual homes are determined by our ruling love. We are drawn, irresistibly, to communities of like-hearted beings—heaven for those who love good and truth, hell for those who love self above all else. In other words, we are not placed in heaven or hell—we gravitate there because we become the quality we love.

The Golden Rule is, therefore, a perfect law of spiritual attraction. By practising it sincerely—not for reward, but because it reflects the reality we want to live in—we begin to manifest that reality. We align with the heavenly order of selfless love and usefulness.

In daily life and from a practical perspective, the Golden Rule challenges us at every turn. Consider:

- When someone speaks harshly to you: Do you react with equal force, or do you respond with truth and gentleness, showing the kind of response you would wish for when *you* are having a bad day?
- In conflict: Do you seek to "win," or to understand and uplift?
- In generosity: Do you give because it reflects the kind of world you wish existed, or because you want to be praised for giving?
- In judgement: Do you assume intent based on action, or do you offer the same benefit of the doubt you would hope to receive?

Each of these moments is a seed. The Golden Rule, applied not from ego but from insight, cultivates the ground of your spirit.

The Golden Rule encapsulates the entire movement of spiritual regeneration. It is a formula for:

- Putting truth into action (wisdom)
- Prioritising use over ego
- Forming heaven in our hearts

It is the bridge between understanding and being. As Swedenborg describes, the will is the essence of a person, and the understanding is its form. The Golden Rule is the harmonious union of both: willing the good of another through thoughtful action.

To live by this rule is to live in alignment with heaven.

And as we align our internal quality with this eternal law, we draw ourselves—spiritually and irresistibly—toward the societies of heaven that live by it.

A final thought:

If all humanity sincerely lived by the Golden Rule, we would not need any other laws. Not because the rule is simplistic, but because it contains within it the seed of all true religion, all true love, and all true wisdom.

It is not a rule of fairness, but a rule of formation:

"As you sow, so shall you reap."

Galatians 6:7

The Golden Rule is not merely advice for polite society —it is the blueprint for life.

Let us then treat each moment with the reverence it deserves, for every act toward another is a step toward who we are becoming.

Time

"The time is fulfilled, and the kingdom of God is at hand."

Mark 1:5

Since we are dealing with spiritual realities, time and space need to be touched on.

Some people believe that time is an actual thing, that it exists in and of itself independently. Spurred on by many movies talking about time travel, people postulate or fantasise about travelling back in time or through time. We say that something exists in time, in history. And as if it's an actual tangible thing, we say time heals. Is this so? I suggest that time is something entirely different.

While temporal distortions and time travel makes for very interesting fantasy, I tell you that time is merely a unit of measurement. To say it differently: a measurement of progress. Just like: centimeters, kilometers, liters and other units that describe a particular measurement of something. *Time*, in terms of hours, days or minutes does not actually exist. In the same way that a centimeter or a meter (ie space) does not exist. Yes, we can look at the earth revolving around the sun travelling through the universe, but this simply means we can see progress or progression: a linear progression.

And that is exactly what time as a unit describes: progress. It only exists because we are able to progress, to change. We are only able to measure progress because progress exists. Progress does not exist on account of time existing. It's the other way around: time exists on account of our finality and ability to change. In other words, time is the effect and result of progress and our changing projection!

This is no different than saying travelling through space and time is the result of our changing states of mind and therefore the world 'around us'.

Change directly correlates to our shifts in states and once you realise this, some of the biblical stories also come alive. For example, Moses going up and down the mountain, Jonah being swallowed by a large fish, Noah in his Ark or the paralytic being command to get up from his bed and walk.

These all talk to (spiritual) states of mind we can find ourselves in. You may have also heard said that we are not physical beings having a 'spiritual' experience, but spirits having a 'physical' experience. This is very true and the reality of this, once you understand it, is mind-blowing and eye opening.

Therefore, we experience and are able to measure time as a result of experiencing spiritual change. Perhaps that is now obvious and self-evident? We are finite beings and so have a beginning, and ultimately have (or experience) an end in one way or another. While we may have infinite potential, we are clearly not infinite. Unlike our creator: The source of all that is.

The infinite a-priori, Who exists in and of Himself, therefore is outside of time and space, and therefore does not progress (or in another word: 'change').

The infinite source is always and forever the same. The cause, the ultimate cause. We are the effects. We are created. We are the result of something and we have a beginning. And as result of having a beginning we have finality (ie growth or development) and so progression towards whatever is.

That progress is spiritual - being the developing of our mind (or to use a different term: character). We learn and grow in understanding. It's really all about the growing of our mind, changing our mind. So time is, if you really think about it, and as it does not exist independently, just a measure.

To add a parting comment to this: time is not an agent of change - nothing is changed or caused by waiting any period of time. Saying something is more feasible or likely because of a longer period of time is nonsensical and absurd. It is not the time, but the changes happening over time that must have a real cause, as time is merely an effect and no cause of anything.

I hate to spoil the plot of many fascinating movies, but we cannot travel 'through' time. Only the now exists! Once the now passes it no longer is and so you can never again be.

We cannot actually go 'back' to what isn't. There is only progress, a proceeding from the Divine. Not a regression or recession into the Infinite. It is logically impossible.

The closest thing you can get to time travel technically, is to get a visual image from something that has occurred in the past in the now, like a memory. This is no different than having a photograph. There is no way of interacting with it, because it doesn't actually exist in the now.

And before you ask, no - there are also no multiple 'timelines' operating independently from each other, where our 'duplicates' are living an alternate reality. As we learned, there is, and can be, only One reality!

3 Keys to Spiritual Growth

"If you want to be perfect, go, sell what you have and give to the poor, and you will have treasure in heaven; and come, follow Me."

Matthew 19:21

To find true meaning and purpose in your spiritual life I will share the three critical elements all true spiritual leaders have in common! These are the fundamental and key elements required for a meaningful and effective spiritual practice and thus finding true purpose in your life. Or to say it differently, three key requirements you must have in place if you want your spiritual life and path to enlightenment to be successful and have a spiritual practise that actually works.

Without these three elements – in other words if one is missing – you will find it impossible to attain a peaceful state of mind and find purposeful direction to your life. Without just one of these three elements your spiritual practise will never result in true inner transformation. I can attest to that from over twenty years of practical experience.

So, let us start here with the first key requirement:

1. Love what is good

Of course we begin by addressing the heart. Our heart is at the very centre of any spiritual growth, because it defines who we are now and dictates who we wish to become. Without changing what we love, we cannot progress and improve our inner character and true nature.

You need the will to change and engage in honest introspection (being critical self-assessment), which in

Christian terms is referred to as repentance.

Scripture tells us to Love the Lord your God and to love the neighbour as yourself. It tells us to help others, be useful and to do good. Scripture too tells us that we are what we love and this teaching is also core to Swedenborgian spiritual philosophy.

You need to unpack your own affections – your deepest and most fundamental loves and then seek to battle and reduce those that relate to selfish desires. Scripture often refers to evil and evils, but to make these terms more meaningful, perhaps even more practical and personal, they can be replaced with selfishness and selfish desires, which are synonymous. You see, it is not an external battle we are called on, a battle for us to point the finger to the outside world and identify how bad and unfair it is.

No, we are called to the battle within, it is our inner world and battleground where this fight is fought. Where our transformation takes place and the spiritual warrior must rule.

Perhaps it is for another lesson to delve deeper into this, but selfishness stems from an intrinsic level of self-love that seeks to dominate and rule over others. It does not have to be full blown narcissism or egotism on display, because at its foundation – its ultimate core - it simply is an unhealthy prioritisation of self and thinking we have are the ultimate source of our own life and intellect. This is why many self-help gurus and new age feel good programs can be so destructive when they seek to affirm and prioritise our love for self. I wholeheartedly believe that in the truest sense self-love is never something we lack, ever!

OK, so what is good and why do we need to love it?

Well this requires acceptance that there is such a thing as good and evil. This means we need to accept an objective reality and moral absolute. For me therefore, to summarise it for you in simple terms, good can be determined on a number of characteristics:

- It is in harmony with and affirmative of objective reality; meaning it exists and supports something real – not imaginary

- It therefore also supports or underpins what is true.

- It then also limitless or supports a continuation of its existence or effect.

- Therefore it is outward focused and it is the opposite of self-serving – meaning it gives, rather than takes – it creates, rather than consumes

- Finally, it is thus productive and of use, seeking to serve and be of continued use. The opposite of being destructive, which consumption is.

Love is equated with willing something to be and as such is a creative force. To love what is good, then, in simple terms is willing to be of use and seeking to sustain what is spiritually productive. In other words, we must seek to serve, love others, be productive and be self-less.

Now let us move to the second key requirement:

2. Love what is true

Addressing the head – you need the understanding to change and so engage in mindful discernment. In other words, you need wisdom!

For this we may study the Word through the Sacred Scriptures, like the Bible, Gita or Koran.

You need to unpack your beliefs through rationality and logic, and carefully consider the things that are objectively so – not because we want them to be true. We need to minimise our false thinking.

We must have the humility too to accept that knowledge and wisdom originates outside of ourselves, that we do not have all the answers within us. We must again accept that there is such a thing as truth – objective reality.

The reason for us to support this, first and foremost, is

because we do not wish to delude ourselves and live in a fantasy world. At some point, we will be confronted with the consequences of our actions and beliefs and thus the sooner we comply with reality, the better. In other words, we cannot deny reality nor its effects.

Reality is greater than ourselves. By accepting what is true, we support something bigger than us. We submit to it and accept our place in it. The opposite is to fight it, seek to control it and delude ourselves to be the only reality that matters. That is not the road to peace and enlightenment.

Truth is light and accepting the truth, to the best of our ability, is to enlighten our minds. This is a continuous process of improvement. As our understanding grows, we must be willing to re-prioritise, reorder and restructure our thinking. We must reconsider the consequences and our fundamentals based on newfound knowledge and understanding.

Scripture tells us not to lean on our own understanding. It tells us that the Divine is the Way and the Light. In other words, objective reality itself and Wisdom itself. That is what we must accept and it is with this humility and open mind that we find what we seek on our spiritual quest.

If we don't prioritise what is true in our lives, we are effectively lying to ourselves and denying ourselves a life in harmony with reality.

After we have focused on the heart space to ensure we actually wish to change our affections towards what is good and true AND we focus our attention on the cognitive part of our mind to understand and learn what is true - the time follows to put it into practise!

Therefore the third critical component of any effective and transformative spiritual practise is.

3. Act on it (being useful)

Knowledge and feelings are useless – left to be just imaginary in our heads alone – unless we put what we know to be good and true into practise. Change is only effected when we ourselves choose to own and apply it. This is a process involving our own volition, our heart – and so that is why personal freedom is so critical to actual spiritual transformation and enlightenment! You may wish to refer to the earlier chapter on *Freedom.*

At risk of stating the obvious, but it cannot hurt reiterating that we need to make sure that our hearts and minds operate in harmony with each other. That what we believe to be true is acted on from a love within ourselves for what is true. We need to make sure – when given the chance and opportunity – to enact on our newfound knowledge and so strengthen our affection for truth.

This is the final, but critical component if we are to grow and change our character. We cannot win the inner battle for peace unless our hearts and mind are in harmony with each other. We are not truly free unless we act out our loves in our lives.

It is easy to delude ourselves into thinking that only believing a particular teaching is enough or that it doesn't matter that I am doing a kindness for others for selfish reasons. It is very easy for us to behave in a way or say things contrary to our thinking and simply justify our discrepancies away and too many people do.

This lesson is the most critical, because it deals with our core integrity. This is where the rubber hits the road and we pass the test or fail.

Scripture tells us we should act on the opportunities we have to do good, be kind and choose truth. Swedenborg tells us that if we do not act on what we believe, we ultimately fail to believe it no matter how much we have convinced ourselves to think we do. If we don't act upon what we think we know and love, we do not actually love it! That is the simple truth.

You see, this brings up a key problem and why a great many people fail on their spiritual quest! It takes real and deep introspection, personal analysis with sincerity and persistence, to grow. It is self-critical, it is painful and hard work to acknowledge our wrongs our selfish affections. Especially since everything in the world seeks to sell us an easy way out. Seeks to tell us we are good enough.

Well, we are NOT and once you understand the nature of reality and our reality - once you truly understand the real purpose in your life - this illusion of autonomy and self-importance remains mighty appealing, but will ultimately fail to bring you lasting happiness and freedom from your inner struggle.

This is why many people jump to the next fashionable spiritual trend, such as meditation, mindfulness or hot yoga, but find no real difference in their lives. You see there are two issues to understand with this:

1. People mistake engaging in an external activity with being spiritual; and

2. Expect the thin veneer of calm the activity brings to be lasting and transformational.

This is why meditation, yoga, mindfulness and the like do NOT work. They only work when and because people apply and accept the three critical elements I have discussed in this series!

True and lasting change only comes when we rebuild our paradigms and put our whole self in!

Community support

It is all well and good knowing – understanding – these critical elements all of us need for our spiritual practise to be truly effective – truly transformative. To know what ALL true spiritual leaders past, present and future have in common in their spiritual practise.

If we are to develop a heavenly character and gain a

lasting sense of calm and peace, indeed we must love what is good, love what is true and apply it to our lives – act on it. We need to live it, embed it into our life! However, it is mighty difficult doing this by ourselves, alone. We all need friends. What we need is community support.

To bring it all together and support your application in life of newfound principles - to support your personal spiritual practise and cycle of life, with new discovery, introspection and personal growth – we can all benefit from having a group of friends to support us and who know what we need and go through.

No, I am not talking about just another echo chamber that is merely re-affirming our old beliefs, but an environment that positively challenges and supports us in our quest for enlightenment. I see many people that are part of spiritual communities in real life or participate in various groups on social media that match their current belief system.

While it is not necessary for us to maintain our mere comfort zone and seek to reaffirm our own thoughts and beliefs – remember our ego, with its selfish affections and fundamental love of self, seeks to justify itself in the most subtle ways continuously – so, we can – and many do – simply stay stagnant and affirm their stasis. They do not grow or engage in true spiritual transformation.

What we need is to actively seek out our personal tasks in our inner spiritual work to grow. We need to challenge ourselves constantly with new spiritual light and in active application of our newfound principles. We need to support one another in this struggle, not merely reaffirm platitudes and false praise telling ourselves we are so good!

We all need friends in our spiritual battles.

How to Read the Bible

"Did not our heart burn within us while He talked with us on the road, and while He opened the Scriptures to us?"

Luke 24:32

You might be surprised that there are more than one way to read anything, let alone the sacred scriptures. I believe there is a traditional, a practical and a spiritual way to read the scriptures. Let me here briefly outline the three distinctly different ways of reading the scriptures as I see it.

1. Traditionally

One may also call this the literal or natural method. This method is aimed at the literal text alone and is useful for memorising stories, finding references and learning historical context. It is a way to enjoy the prose and beauty of the language upon which much of Shakespeare is based too. This method helps us predominantly builds up stories for recalling at a later time from our memory.

It particularly applies when reading the scriptures cover-to-cover, such as daily bible reading programs or presenting bible stories to children. The same applies when we listen to audio bibles or when we watch a video based on biblical stories. It is no different to the way we read any novel for entertainment or seek to gain any knowledge for the sake of knowing.

Here is a bible verse many will know from having memorised it:

> *"If anyone thirsts, let him come to Me and drink. He who believes in Me, as the Scripture has said, out of his heart will flow rivers of living water."*
>
> John 7:37-38

I think, well I hope, you can agree with me that reading scripture in this way has a place, but presents a very limited path. It puts all the responsibility on the text to present itself and this method offers no deeper an approach than mere memory knowledge.

2. Practically

The practical method is not directly aimed at the literal text alone, but focuses on personal guidance for life application. It seeks to find rules to follow or examples of life application and may therefore also be called the application method.

It applies when we infer character qualities from biblical figures, draw on proverbs, laws and sayings on how to live and follow direct examples or rules taught in various places. Looking for practical support in the sacred scriptures sees an extra layer of meaning and effect coming from the various biblical stories.

You can see there is a personal level of interpretation required with how to give effect to the practical advice derived from the literal text in sacred scripture. This is possibly too the level at which most misunderstanding and conflict occurs as a result of doctrinal application differences.

Here is a bible verse we refer to as the Golden rule. This same law is found in every religion in one form or another.

> *"In everything, therefore, treat people the same way you want them to treat you, for this is the Law and the*

Prophets."

Matthew 7:12 (NASB)

Perhaps you can see somewhat of a progression?

As we look to practical application, the actual literal text becomes a little less important beyond the guidance it offers informing the interpretation. This must by necessity be so, because not all text is absolute and without any ambiguity. Reason being is that language is contextual and dependent on cultural norms and to lesser extent personal interpretation from experience.

3. Spiritually

This method is seemingly the most contentious, because it mostly disregards the meaning of the literal text, but focuses on direct personal application. It can also be referred to as the symbolic or allegorical method and with it separates the interpreted meaning from the literal meaning, it should not be considered arbitrarily.

Within this there are essentially two distinct sub-methods:

A. The allegorical interpretation in which there is a consistent level of representation (or correspondence) between the natural presentation and the spiritual meaning that underpins it. For example, it is well known (on the most rudimentary level of allegory) that by light or to see is actually meant to understand and that by taking up the cross is not meant to literally carry a heavy wooden structure, but to take responsibility for our character and behaviour and so doing what we must.

B. The personal interpretation in which we meditate and pray to understand the personal message the Word has for us. It seeks to gain insight for spiritual correction and is the only method by which we have a direct connection with the Lord.

Only these two related ways of approaching the sacred scripture spiritually carry the mechanism by which The Lord is actually acknowledged as the Living Word. In other words, where the Word is allowed to live in us.

The following verse offers a great example of where the Bible itself gives us insight into it's living spiritual nature.

> *"And beginning at Moses and all the Prophets, He expounded to them in all the Scriptures the things concerning Himself... And they said to one another, 'Did not our heart burn within us while He talked with us on the road, and while He opened the Scriptures to us?'"*
>
> Luke 24:27,32

I wholeheartedly recommend studying the allegorical nature of the sacred scriptures, as well as take time to regularly meditate and allow The Word through the scriptures offer you guidance in this way.

A final note

Before leaving you with the idea that these methods of approaching the way you read the sacred scriptures are exclusive, as well as distinct, allow me to make it clear to you that, while the deeper allegorical meaning may be totally removed from what presents on the surface level and therefore seemingly unconnected, in the ideal circumstance it will be true on all levels at the same time. However we must constantly bear in mind that the Lord (the Word) is in fact only considered with our spiritual character - our heart and not so much with what we do or know.

This is also how you will find the distinction between biblical text useful for teaching and those parts that I believe can actually be considered the Word. The Word, which is infinite and complete, must be consistent and true on the spiritual level first and foremost: the cause of our reality. If you look for it, you will find a consistent correspondence between the natural and the spiritual. This is the Law of Correspondence and magical once you get to understand it.

> *"By faith we understand that the worlds were framed by the word of God, so that the things which are seen were not made of things which are visible."*
>
> Hebrews 11:3

12 tips to read the Bible for meaning

1. Context - read section before and after.
2. Use an accurate translation that is true to the original meaning.
3. Compare translations, and do not simply use one version only.
    - Include a trans-literal version for comparison (a version where the same word is always translated exactly the same)
4. Use a highlighter and mark your bible! It is a tool for learning and application, so use it!
5. Focus and remove distractions - make sure the atmosphere is conducive to learning.
6. Expect to receive and be open to what comes up.
7. Compare what is happening in passages that have a similar theme.
8. Don't hunt for preconceived ideas. Avoid subtly reading our own will in the scripture for self-justification.
    - In other words, do not tell the word what is says, but allow the word to speak.
    - We can justify anything from scripture by focusing on specific verses or ever so subtly adjust our interpretation.
9. Avoid mixing the levels or ways you are reading:

natural historical, practical instruction or spiritual instruction.
- Do not expect all levels to hold true at the same time.
- Cease to expect the Bible to be a historical book. It is a spiritual manual.
- You could add "in me" to each sentence, to ask what process is being described for you - right now!

10. Study the allegorical language and ancient symbolism to unpack the deeper truths for personal spiritual application.
11. Look for and draw out the broader theme by describing what is occurring in the most general sense possible.
    - Moving up the mountain: an aspect of elevation.
    - Moving to a different city, travelling: a state of transition
12. Study together with others to hold yourself accountable and to enhance learning through discussion and sharing.

* * *

Key Terminology

Ruling love – the dominant affection shaping a person's spirit.

Use/Usefulness – acting from love and truth for others' good.

Correspondence – spiritual meaning behind natural imagery.

Law of attraction (spiritual) – "like is drawn to like" principle.

Internal / external Church – presence of good & truth vs institutional form.

Golden Rule – Matthew 7:12 as universal spiritual law.

Regeneration – lifelong spiritual rebirth process.

Will & Understanding – twin faculties of the mind.

Divine Love & Wisdom – essential aspects of God and reality.

Reference Sources

Swedenborg, E. 1911–12, Apocalypse Explained (Standard edn), trans. J C Ager, rev. J Whitehead, Swedenborg Foundation, New York.

Swedenborg, E. 1983–99, Arcana Coelestia (Secrets of Heaven), 8 vols, trans. J Elliott, Swedenborg Society, London. (New Christian Bible Study)

Swedenborg, E. 1918, Canons of the New Church, trans. J F Potts, Swedenborg Society, London.

Swedenborg, E. 1995, Charity: The Practice of Neighbourliness, 2nd edn, trans. W F Wunsch, ed. W R Woofenden, Swedenborg Foundation, West Chester PA.

Swedenborg, E. 1995, Conjugial Love (Delights of Wisdom Relating to Conjugial Love), trans. N B (Bruce) Rogers, General Church of the New Jerusalem, Bryn Athyn PA. (New Christian Bible Study)

Swedenborg, E. 2014, Doctrine of Faith (in Life / Faith, Portable New Century Edn), trans. G F Dole, Swedenborg Foundation, West Chester PA. (Biblio)

Swedenborg, E. 2014, Doctrine of Life (in Life / Faith, Portable New Century Edn), trans. G F Dole, Swedenborg Foundation, West Chester PA. (Biblio)

Swedenborg, E. 2015, Sacred Scripture / White Horse (New Century Edn), trans. G F Dole, Swedenborg Foundation, West Chester PA. (All Bookstores)

Reference Sources

Swedenborg, E. 2003, Divine Love and Wisdom, Portable New Century Edn, trans. G F Dole, Swedenborg Foundation, West Chester PA.

Swedenborg, E. 2010, Divine Providence, Portable New Century Edn, rev. edn, trans. G F Dole, Swedenborg Foundation, West Chester PA.

Swedenborg, E. 2000, Heaven and Hell, New Century Edn, trans. G F Dole, Swedenborg Foundation, West Chester PA. (New Century Edition)

Swedenborg, E. 2007, New Jerusalem and Its Heavenly Doctrine (in Shorter Works of 1763), trans. J S Rose, Swedenborg Foundation, West Chester PA.

Swedenborg, E. 2010–11, True Christianity, vols 1–2, trans. J S Rose, Swedenborg Foundation, West Chester PA.

For more information on Emanuel Swedenborg - and all publications - visit www.swedenborg.com

For more information:
www.freedomphilosophy.life

"..you shall know the truth, and the truth shall make you free."
John 8:32

Freedom Philosophy promotes a meaningful spirituality, teaching the essential practices of an effective spiritual life using ancient principles. When practised, these spiritual principles help us to free our minds, grow in wisdom, discover our purpose and strengthen our faith and connection with the Divine.

www.ingramcontent.com/pod-product-compliance
Lightning Source LLC
Chambersburg PA
CBHW031250290426
44109CB00012B/517